TOP *Male* Christian Artists

FEATURING 25
CONTEMPORARY CHRISTIAN HITS

COMPILED AND EDITED BY
BRYCE INMAN

Contents

Dive

Recorded by Steven Curtis Chapman

Words and Music by
STEVEN CURTIS CHAPMAN

9
A♭maj7
B♭
they've carved their way to where the wild and rush - ing riv - er can be found.
It can bring the dead to life and it can fill an emp - ty soul
11
A♭maj7
B♭
And like the rain, I have been car - ried here to where the riv - er flows,
and give our heart the on - ly thing worth liv - ing and worth dy - ing for,
13
Cno3
F
E♭
A♭maj7
yeah.
yeah.
15
B♭
My heart is rac - ing and my knees are weak as I walk to the edge.
But we will nev - er know the awe-some pow - er of the grace of God

17 A♭maj7
B♭
I know there is no turn - ing back a - once my feet have left the ledge.
un - til we let our - selves get swept a - way in - to this ho - ly flood.
19 A♭maj7
B♭
And in the rush, I hear a voice that's tell - ing me it's time to take
So if you take my hand, we'll close our eyes and count to three and take
21 A♭maj7
Gno3
Cno3
Gno3
f
the leap of faith, so here I go. I'm div - ing in; I'm go - ing deep,
the leap of faith. Come on, let's go.
23 Am7
Fno3
Gno3
Cno3
Gno3
in o - ver my head. I wan - na be caught in the rush, lost in the flow.

25 Am7
Fno3
Gno3
Cno3
Gno3
In o - ver my head I wan - na go. The riv - er's deep; the riv - er's wide;
27 Am7
Fno3
Gno3
A♭
B♭2(no3)
the riv - er's wa - ter is a - live, so sink or swim, I'm div - ing in.
1.
29 Cno3
F2(no3)
mf
31 Cno3
F2(no3)

33
F
E♭
C
F
E♭
A♭maj7
2.
35
C
G
mf
F
I'm div - ing in.
37
C
Oh,
G
F
I'm div - ing in,
39
C
G
F
yeah, hah.
I'm div - ing in,

41
C
yeah.
G
F
Here I
go.
43
F
E♭
C
F
E♭
A♭maj7
46
F
E♭
C
F
E♭
A♭maj7
(♮)
49
f
Come on,
let's
go.
Cno3
Gno3
(♮)
I'm
div - ing in;
I'm
go - ing deep,
f

51 Am7 Fno3 Gno3 Cno3 Gno3
in o - ver my head. I wan - na be caught in the rush, lost in the flow.
53 Am7 Fno3 Gno3 Cno3 Gno3
In o - ver my head I wan - na go. The riv - er's deep; the riv - er's wide;
55 Am7 Fno3 Gno3
the riv - er's wa - ter is a - live,
1. A♭ B♭2(no3)
so sink or swim, I'm div - ing in.
57 2. A♭ B♭2(no3) A♭ Gno3
so sink or swim, I'm div - ing in. So sink or swim, I'm div - ing in.

59
A♭
B♭2(no3)
So sink or swim,
I'm div - ing in.
61
Cno3
Gno3
Am7
Fno3
Gno3
Woh
63
Cno3
Gno3
1.
Am7
Fno3
Gno3
Woh
I'm div - ing in.
65
2.
Am7
Fno3
Gno3
Cno3
I'm div - ing in.
I'm div - ing in.

The Power of a Moment

Recorded by Chris Rice

Words and Music by
CHRIS RICE

8
E
A
what are they gon - na write a - bout me when I'm gone?
10
F♯
A
These are the ques - tions that shape the way I think a - bout what mat -
12
B
E
- ters. Well, I have no guar - an - tee of my next heart -
14
A
B
- beat. My world's too big to make a name

16
A
for my - self; and what if no one wants to read a - bout me
E
18
A
when I'm gone?
F♯
It seems to me that right
20
A
now's the on - ly mo - ment that mat - ters.
F♯
22
A
You know the num - ber of my days,
E

24
A
E
so come paint Your pic - tures on the can - vas in my head and
26
A
C♯m
come write Your wis - dom on my heart.
And teach me the
28
F♯
A
pow - er of a mo - ment,
the pow - er of a mo - ment,
2nd time to CODA
30
F♯
A
the pow - er of a mo - ment.

32
E
A
E
2. In Your king - dom where the least is great -
35
A
B
- est,
the weak are giv - en strength and fools con -
37
A
E
found the wise,
and for - ev - er brush - es up a - gainst a
39
A
F♯
mo - ment's time,
leav - ing im - press - ions and

41
A
F♯
D.S. al CODA 𝄋
draw - ing me in - to what real - ly mat - ters.
𝄌 CODA
43
A
E
the pow - er of a mo - ment.
45
B
F♯m7
I get so dis - tract - ed by my big - ger schemes.
47
B
F♯m
Show me the im - por - tance of the sim - ple things like a word,

49
a seed, a thorn, a nail and a cup of cold wa - ter.
51
C♯
A
You know the num - ber of my
53
E
A
days, so come paint Your pic - tures on the can -
55
E
A
- vas in my head and come write Your wis - dom on my heart.

57
C♯m
F♯
And teach me the pow - er of a mo - ment,
1.
59
A
F♯
the pow - er of a mo - ment.
2.
61
A
F♯
the pow - er of a mo - ment,
63
A
the pow - er of, the pow - er of, the pow - er of the mo -

65
E
A
- ment,
yeah.

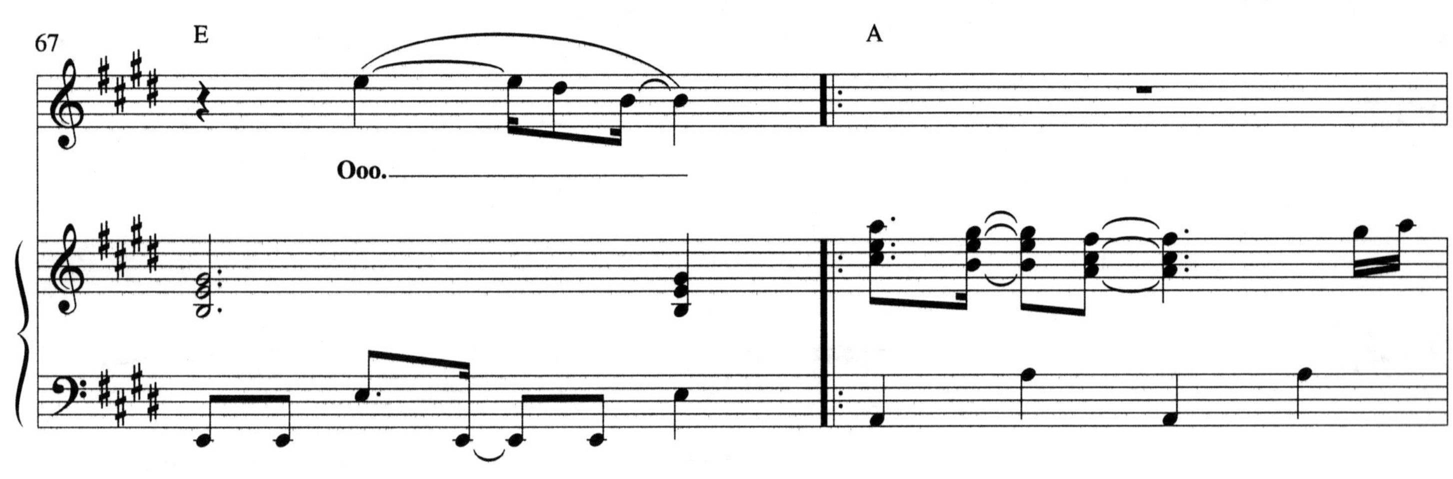
67
E
A
Ooo.

69
E
Repeat and ad lib.
A
E

Love Me Good

Recorded by Michael W. Smith

Words and Music by
MICHAEL W. SMITH and
WAYNE KIRKPATRICK

10
C2(no3)
G
C2(no3)
G
C2(no3)
G
Yeah, life is a three - ring cir - cus with clowns and freaks and cam - els and such,
12
C2(no3)
G
C2(no3)
G
C2(no3)
G
you nev - er know when you might be at - tacked by the bears.
14
Em
D/E
Em
D/E
Em
Bm7
C
Am7
D/A
Em/A
Am7
D/A
Em/A
Give me love, give me love, love me good. Give me love, give me love,
17
D
Dsus
G
Em
D/E
Em
D/E
Em
Bm7
C
love me good. Give me love, give me love, love me good.

20
Am7
D/A
Em/A
Am7
D/A
Em/A
D
Dsus
G
Give me love, give me love, love me good. La la la la la
22
C2(no3)
G
C2(no3)
G
C2(no3)
G
la love me good.
24
C2(no3)
G
C2(no3)
G
C2(no3)
G
26
C2(no3)
G
C2(no3)
G
C2(no3)
G
mf
2. Some - times I feel like I'm a - fraid of my own shad - ow and then,

28
C2(no3)
G
C2(no3)
G
C2(no3)
G
some - times I can feel as bold as Gen - ghis Khan.
30
C2(no3)
G
C2(no3)
G
C2(no3)
G
But, I could nev - er live in a yurt on a di - et of Mon - go - li - an bar - be - cue,
32
C2(no3)
G
C2(no3)
G
C2(no3)
G
I con - quer the world for a mo - ment then the mo - ment is gone.
34
Em
D/E
Em
D/E
Em
Bm7
C
Am7
D/A
Em/A
Am7
D/A
Em/A
Give me love, give me love, love me good.
Give me love, give me love,

37
D Dsus G
Em D/E Em D/E Em Bm7 C
love me good.
Give me love, give me love, love me good.
40
Am7 D/A Em/A Am7 D/A Em/A
1. D Dsus G
2. D Dsus G
Give me love, give me love, love me good.
love me good.
43
C2(no3) G C2(no3) G C2(no3) G
45
C2(no3) G C2(no3) G C2(no3) G

47
C Cm B Bm Em7 Em6 A7 D7sus G
Let us take a mo - ment now to bow our heads and
50
C Cm6 B Bm7 Em7 A7 D7sus
pray, if on - ly to give thanks for mak - ing it through
53
G C2(no3) G C2(no3) G
an - oth - er day. Some - times I wish I was in a mov -
55
C2(no3) G C2(no3) G C2(no3) G
ie or some sev - en - ties T V thing where ev - 'ry - thing gets neat - ly wrapped by the

57
C2(no3)
G
C2(no3)
G
C2(no3)
G
end of the show.
Yeah, but this ain't Hol - ly - wood and
59
C2(no3)
G
C2(no3)
G
C2(no3)
G
this sure ain't the Bra - dy Bunch, and
how this plot's gon - na all pan out I
61
C2(no3)
G
Em
D
E
Em
D
E
Em
Bm7
C
don't real - ly know.
Give me love, give me love, love me good.
64
Am7
D
A
Em
A
Am7
D
A
Em
A
D
Dsus
G
Em
D
E
Em
D
E
Em
Give me love, give me love, love me good.
Give me love, give me love,

67
Bm7
C
Am7
D/A
Em/A
Am7
D/A
Em/A
D
Dsus
G
love me good.
Give me love, give me love, love me good.
70
Em
D/E
Em
D/E
Em
Bm7
C
Am7
D/A
Em/A
Am7
D/A
Em/A
Oh, love me good.
Yeah,
73
D
Dsus
G
Em
D/E
Em
D/E
Em
Bm7
C
love me good.
Oh, love me good.
76
Am7
D/A
Em/A
Am7
D/A
Em/A
1.
D
Dsus
G
2.
D
Dsus
G
Yeah, love me good.
love me good. La la la la la

79
C2(no3)
G
C2(no3)
G
C2(no3)
G
la love me good.
Yeah, yeah.
81
C2(no3)
G
C2(no3)
G
C2(no3)
G
C2(no3)
G
C2(no3)
G
Love me, love me, love
84
C2(no3)
G
C2(no3)
G
C2(no3)
G
C2(no3)
G
me good.
87
N.C.
Repeat 3 times and fade
R.H. tacet 1st time

Should've Been Loving You

Recorded by Jonathan Pierce

Words and Music by
TRAVIS MEADOWS and
MIKE LAWLER

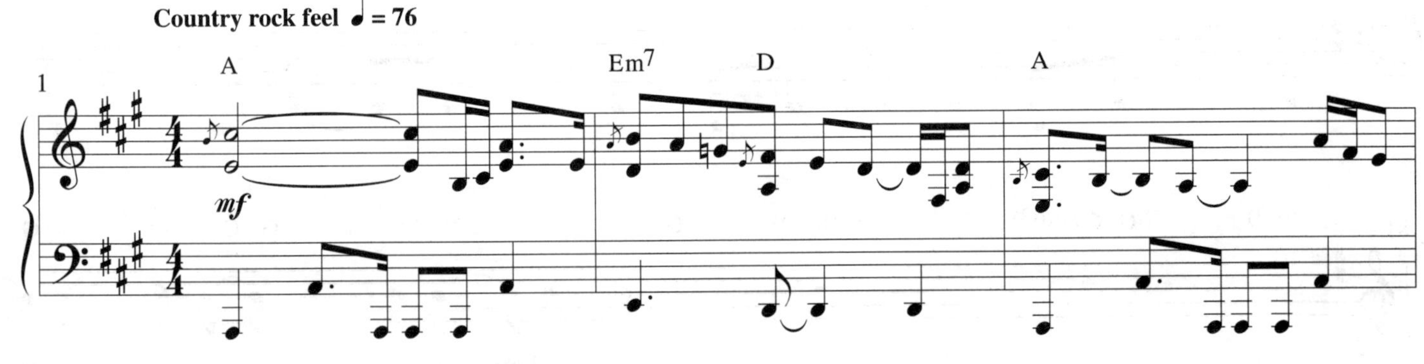

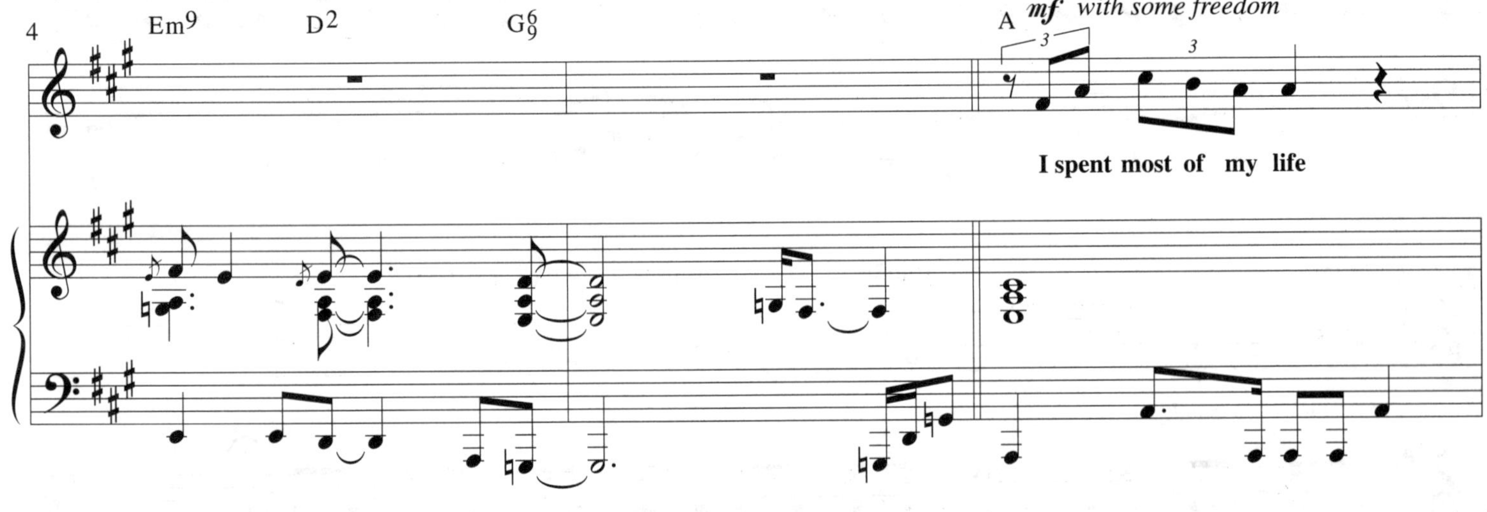

9
D/A A Esus A
I was search - in' for love, I just
11
C♯m7 D
need - ed some af - fec - tion,
all I got just left me want - ing more.
13
D/A A G2
Left me feel - in' cold and lone - ly on the in -
15
A Bm7 A2/C♯
- side with noth - ing to show, but I had

17
G/D
E7sus
f
plen - ty to hide.
I should - 've been lov - in'
19
A
Bm7
You, I should - 've been prais - in' You; should - 've been giv - in' You
f
21
D
A
E7sus
some - thin' in re - turn for the love You've shown.
I should - 've been lov - in'
23
A
Em7
You, should - 've been prais - in' You.
Your

25
D
E
G/D
E7sus
2nd time to Coda
A
love for me was always true,
I should-'ve been lov-in' You.
28
Em7
D
A
Em7
D
31
A
mf
C♯m7
The lone-ly life
does-n't have its ad-van-tag-es,
no, no,
33
D
D/A
A
Esus
it just leaves you hurt-in' all the time.

35
A
C♯m7
And I can safe - ly say
I have found a bet - ter way,
37
D2
D/A
A
it's ac - cept - ance of a great - er kind.
Well, I
39
G2
A
re - mem - ber when Your love came shin - in' in my lone - ly life.
41
Bm7
A2/C♯
G/D
E7sus
D.S. al CODA
Look - in' back on all the love I've thrown a - way,
I re - al - ize
I should - 've been lov - ing

CODA
A
C2
D2/C
No great - er love has
an - y man ev - er known.
D2/E
E2
So that I could live my life, You
Esus
laid down Your own.
Should - 've been lov - in'
Em7
You,
Ooo,
mf

52
D2
A
E7sus
should - 've loved You with all of my life,
yeah.
54
A
Em7
I should - 've been lov - in' You,
I should - 've been prais - in' You.
56
D
E
F
cues: optional
E♭/F
Hey,
Should - 've been lov - in' You,
58
B♭
Cm7
should - 've been prais - in' You;
should - 've been giv - in' You some -

60
E♭
B♭
F7sus
- thin' in re - turn
for the love You've shown.
I should - 've been lov - in' You,
62
B♭
Fm7
E♭
F
should - 've been prais - in' You.
Your love for me was al - ways true,
65
1.
A♭/E♭
F7sus
2.
A♭/E♭
F7sus
I should - 've been lov - in' You,
I should - 've been lov - in' You.
67
B♭
Fm7
E♭
B♭
mp

Can't Get Past the Evidence

Recorded by 4HIM

Words and Music by
MARK HARRIS

10
A
With - out a warn - in' or a sign,
seems You caught me by sur -
But in the midst of ev - 'ry day,
there's a clue, there is a
12
B7
D
B
Bsus
B
- prise;
Now I know the rea - son why:
trace,
a rem - nant of love re - mains,
I'm
15
D
B
Bsus
B
E7
Love is the al - i - bi.
Hey,
yeah!
'Cause I
read - y to rest my case,
hey,
yeah!
18
A(no3)
G2(no3)
F
Esus
can't get past the ev - i - dence,
I can't get past the proof.
I

20
A(no3)
G2(no3)
F
Esus
cue: 2nd time
can't get past the ev - i - dence, it's im - pos - si - ble to do. I
22
1.
A(no3)
G2(no3)
F
Esus
can't get past the ev - i - dence, and I can't de - ny the truth; I
24
D
F
A(no3)
G2(no3)
F
can't get past the ev - i - dence of You, yeah!
27
E
2.
A(no3)
G2(no3)
F
Esus
You are the rea - son that I can't de - ny the truth; I

30
D F A(no3) G2(no3) F
can't get past the ev - i - dence of You, yeah!
33
E Bm7 A/C♯ D D/F♯ E
Be - yond the shad - ow of a doubt I see the light, I'm a vic - tim of a
36
Bm7 A/C♯ D D/F♯ E Bm7 A/C♯ D D/F♯
love I can't de - ny. I'll be the first to tes - ti - fy,
39
E D A G2
yeah, that I can't get past the ev - i - dence of You,

42
Dm/F
E
B(no3)
A2(no3)
yeah! I can't get past the ev - i - dence, I
45
G
F♯sus
B(no3)
A2(no3)
can't get past the proof. I can't get past the ev - i - dence, it's im -
47
G
F♯sus
B(no3)
A2(no3)
pos - si - ble to do. You are the rea - son that I can't
49
G
F♯sus
1.
E
G
de - ny the truth; I can't get past the ev - i - dence. I

51
2.
E
G
B(no3)
A2(no3)
G
F♯
can't get past the ev - i - dence of You,
yeah!
54
B(no3)
A2(no3)
G
F♯sus F♯
B(no3)
A2(no3)
Can't get past the ev - i - dence,
57
G
F♯sus F♯
E
G
F♯
1.
B(no3)
A2(no3)
can't get past the ev - i - dence of You.
60
G
F♯sus F♯
2.
B(no3)

Mercy Said No

Recorded by Greg Long

Words and Music by
DAVE CLARK, DON KOCH and GREG LONG

11
A♭
A♭2(sus)
A♭
for the cause of Christ, I have spent my days be-liev-ing that
13
B♭7sus
B♭m7
E♭7sus
E♭7
what He'd have me be is who I am. As I've
15
Fm
Fm2/E♭
D♭2
D♭
D♭maj7
come to see the weak-er side of me, I've
17
Fm
D♭2
D♭
E♭sus
E♭
re-al-ized His grace is what I need when

19
D♭m/F♭
E♭sus
D♭/E♭
sin de - mand - ed jus - tice for my soul. Mer - cy said, "No,
21
A♭2
Fm7
A♭/E♭
D♭2
A♭2/C
I'm not gon - na let you go. I'm not gon - na let you
23
B♭m7
E♭7sus
B♭m7(♭5)/F♭
B♭m7(♭5)/D♭
slip a - way. You don't have to be a - fraid." Mer - cy said, "No,
25
A♭2
Fm7
A♭/E♭
D♭
A♭2/C
sin will nev - er take con - trol."

27
B♭m7
A♭2/E♭
A♭/E♭
Life and death stood face to face.
Dark - ness tried to steal my heart a - way.
29
B♭/D
B♭
B♭m7(♭5)/F♭
E♭7sus
Thank You, Je - sus.
Mer - cy said, "No."
31
A♭no3
D♭maj9/F
A♭2/C
A♭/C
D♭
E♭
Fm
E♭
mf
2. For
34
A♭2
A♭
E♭7sus/D♭
A♭2/C
A♭/C
God so loved the world that He sent His Son to save us.
From the
mf

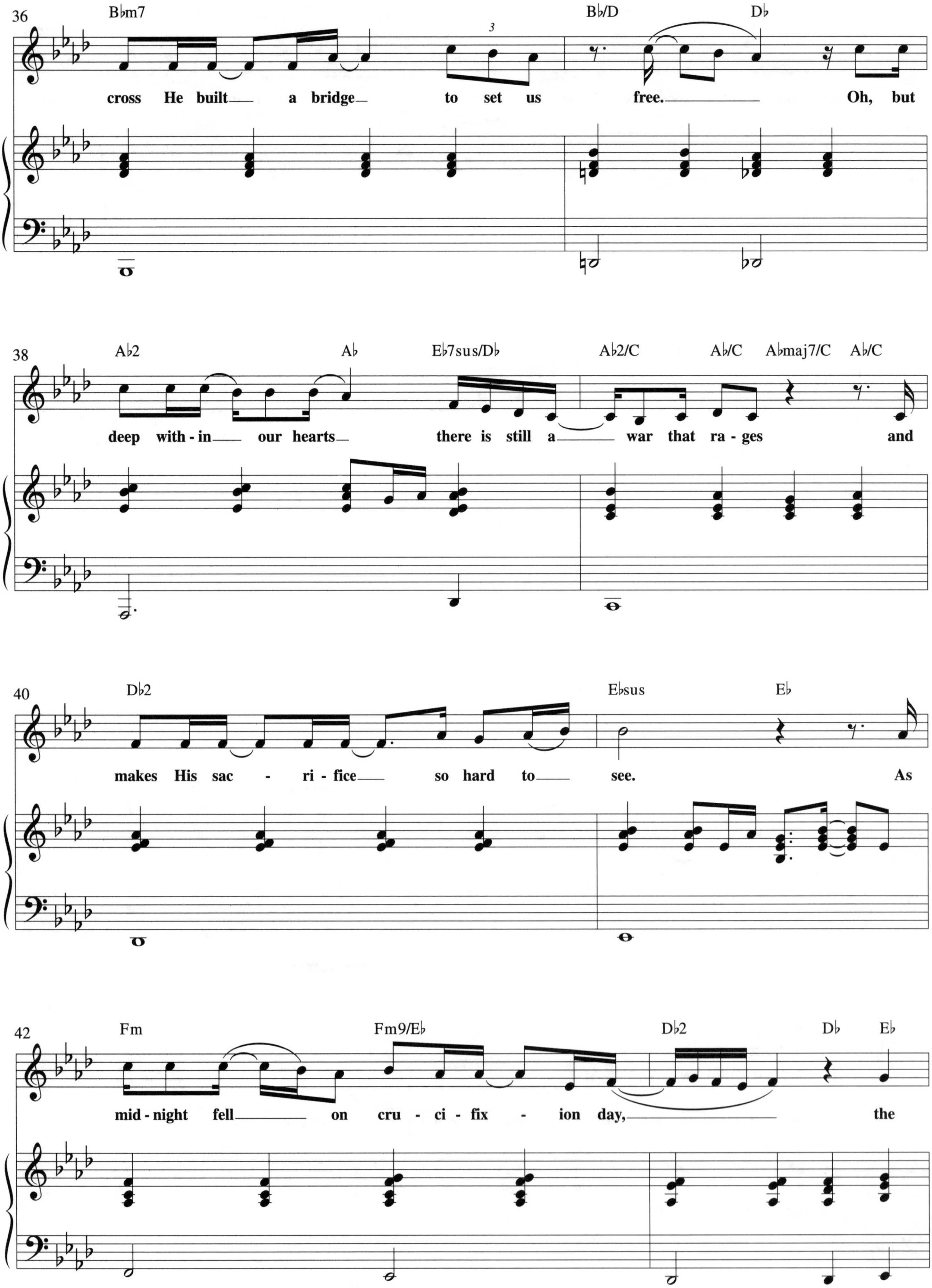

36
B♭m7 B♭/D D♭
cross He built a bridge to set us free. Oh, but
38
A♭2 A♭ E♭7sus/D♭ A♭2/C A♭/C A♭maj7/C A♭/C
deep with - in our hearts there is still a war that ra - ges and
40
D♭2 E♭sus E♭
makes His sac - ri - fice so hard to see. As
42
Fm Fm9/E♭ D♭2 D♭ E♭
mid - night fell on cru - ci - fix - ion day, the

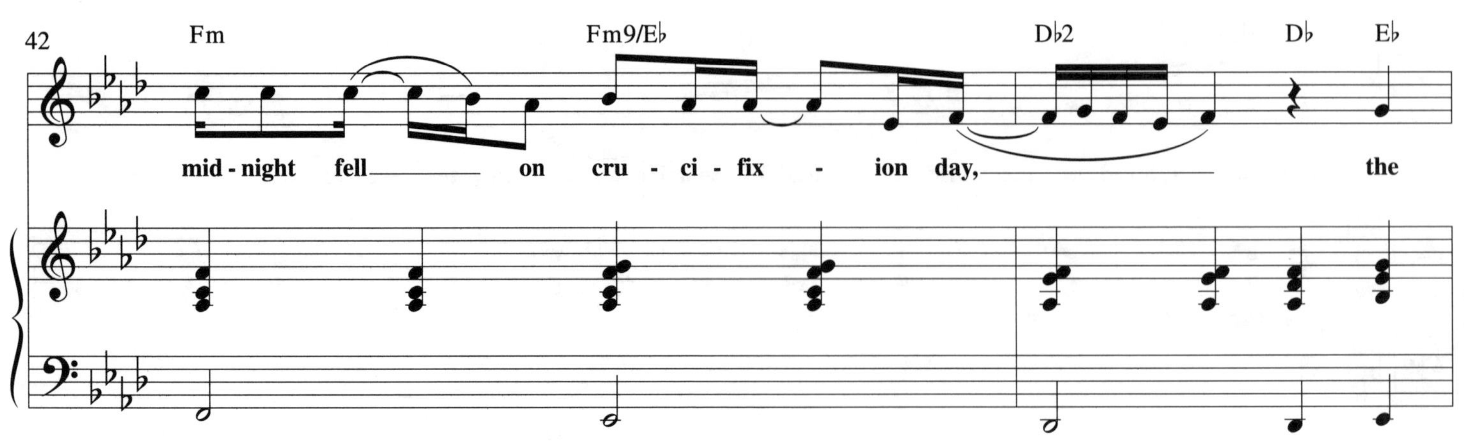

44
Fm
D♭
E♭sus
E♭
light of hope seemed oh so far a - way. And as
46
D♭m/F♭
D♭m
D♭/E♭
e - vil tried to stop re - demp - tion's flow. Mer - cy said, "No,
48
A♭2
Fm7
A♭/E♭
D♭
A♭/C
I'm not gon - na let you go. I'm not gon - na let you
50
B♭m7
E♭7sus
B♭m7(♭5)/F♭
B♭m7(♭5)/D♭
slip a - way. You don't have to be a - fraid." Mer - cy said, "No,

52
A♭2
Fm7
A♭/E♭
D♭
A♭2/C
sin will nev - er take con - trol."
54
B♭m7
A♭2/E♭
A♭/E♭
Life and death stood face to face.
Dark - ness tried to steal my heart a - way.
56
B♭/D
B♭
B♭m7(♭5)/F♭
E♭7sus
A♭
Thank You, Je - sus.
Mer - cy said, "No."
And
59
E♭/G
E♭m/G♭
D♭/F
D♭m/F♭
A♭/E♭
now when heav - en looks at me, it's through the blood of Je - sus, re -

61
B♭/D
B♭
B♭m7(♭5)/F♭
ff
A
mind - ing me of one day, long a - go.
ff
64
Bm7
A2/C♯ A/C♯ D
Bm7(♭5)/F Bm7(♭5)/D
Bm7(♭5)
Mer - cy said, "No,
67
A
F♯m7
A/E
D
A/C♯
I'm not gon - na let you go. I'm not gon - na let you slip
69
Bm7
Bm7/E
Bm7(♭5)/F Bm7(♭5)/D
a - way. You don't have to be a - fraid." Mer - cy said, "No,

71
A
F♯m7
A/C♯
Bm7
A/C♯
sin will nev - er take con - trol."
73
D
A/E
B2/D♯
Life and death stood face to face.
Dark - ness tried to steal my heart a - way.
75
Bm7(♭5)/F
Bm7(♭5)/D
Bm7(♭5)
mf
Thank You, Je - sus. Mer - cy said,
78
Ano3
Dmaj9/F♯
A2/C♯
A/C♯
F♯m7
D2
rit.
D
D/E
A
"No."
Oh.
mf
rit.

Strollin' on the Water

Recorded by Bryan Duncan

Words and Music by
BRYAN DUNCAN and
JOHN ANDREW SCHREINER

13
A
D/A
A
- ed. To see be - yond my - self, be - yond this ti - ny lit - tle world,
15
E
A/E
E7
E
all Your hands have made with beau - ty and strength a -
17
A
D/A
A
lone. I can see You com - in' to me now, Oh,
19
D
Dsus 4/2
D
like a shim - mer - in' light, shim - mer - in' light on an o - pen sea.

21
A
D/A
A
Bare - foot on the wa - ter, laugh - in' at the o - cean like you were old
23
E
friends, call - in' out my name, say - in', "Join me now."
25
A
Bm/A
A
A7
Dsus 4 2
D
Stroll - in' on the wa - ter, high o - ver
28
Dsus 4 2
D
A
Bm/A
A
A7
ev - 'ry care. Stroll - in' on the wa - ter,

31
Dsus4/2 D Fmaj9 Dm/F F♯m
sink - ing no long - er. Let me rise a - bove the
2nd time to Coda
34
A/B B D A/D D
high tide, I can do it, I'll do it, yeah, I know where my strength comes from.
37
A D/A Gmaj7/A A7 Dsus4/2 D Dsus D
Do doot do do. Doot do doot do do. Do doot do do.
41
A D/A A
2. Help me cut these bonds where I keep my spir - it tied down

43
D
Dsus4/2
D
all safe and dry,
safe and dry but so a - fraid.
45
A
D/A
A
Let me come to You,
let me run to You
47
E
A/E
E7
E
while my heart's still beat - ing,
beat - ing in my throat.
49
A
D/A
A
3
With my sweat - y palms and a mouth so dry,
shak - in' 'til I can't

51
D
Dsus4/2
D
stand still. All I'm ask - in', all I'm ask - in' is
53
A
D/A
A
to let me cross that great di - vide be - tween You and I.
55
E
A/E
E
D.S. al CODA
On - ly You can take me there, so take me there, yeah.
CODA
57
D
N.C.
I know that You said, "Fol - low Me." Just let the wa - ter flow; let it go.

60
F♯m
B
B7/D♯
E
Oh, keep your eyes on Me. Do you feel a - live? Try turn - in'
63
A
A7/C♯
D
G
E
E/G♯
A
A/C♯
cir - cles; bend your knees, and hold your hands up high.
66
D
building
D2
D
Can ya feel the wind in your hair? With your eyes closed,
68
Bm7
E/B
Bm7
3
3
take a breath of fresh air, feel the mist on your toes. (Look where we

sing beat one 1st time only
70
E
F♯m/E
E
E7
Asus4/2
A
are.) Stroll - in' on the wa - ter, high o - ver
73
Asus4/2
A
E
F♯m/E
E
E7
ev - 'ry care. Stroll - in' on the wa - ter,
76
Asus4/2
A
1.
Asus4/2
A
2.
Cmaj9
Am/C
sink - ing no long - er. long - er. Let me rise
79
C♯m
E/F♯
F♯
a - bove the high tide, I can

81
A
E/A
A
do it, I'll do it, yeah,
I know where my strength comes from.
83
E
F♯m/E
E
E7
Asus4/2
A
Stroll - in' on the wa - ter,
high o - ver
86
Asus4/2
A
E
F♯m/E
E
E7
ev - 'ry care.
Stroll - in' on the wa - ter,
89
Asus4/2
A
Asus4/2
A
Repeat twice and fade
sink - ing no long - er.

Speechless

Recorded by Steven Curtis Chapman

Words and Music by
STEVEN CURTIS CHAPMAN
and GEOFF MOORE

Joyfully ♩ = 108

1 C G/C F2/C G/C G/F F2 C

p *cresc. poco a poco*

3 G/C F2/C G/C G/F F2

5 C G/C F2/C G/C F2/C F G(add4)/F F F6 F G/C

7 F G(add4)/F F F6 F G/C F G(add4)/F F F6 F G/C

9 F G(add4)/F F F2 C G F2

ff

11
F
G/F
F
G/F
F
G/F
C
G
F2
F
G/F
F

14 C2(no3)
mf
Gno3
1. Words fall like drops of rain;
mf
16 Am
Fno3
C2(no3)
my lips are like clouds.
I say so

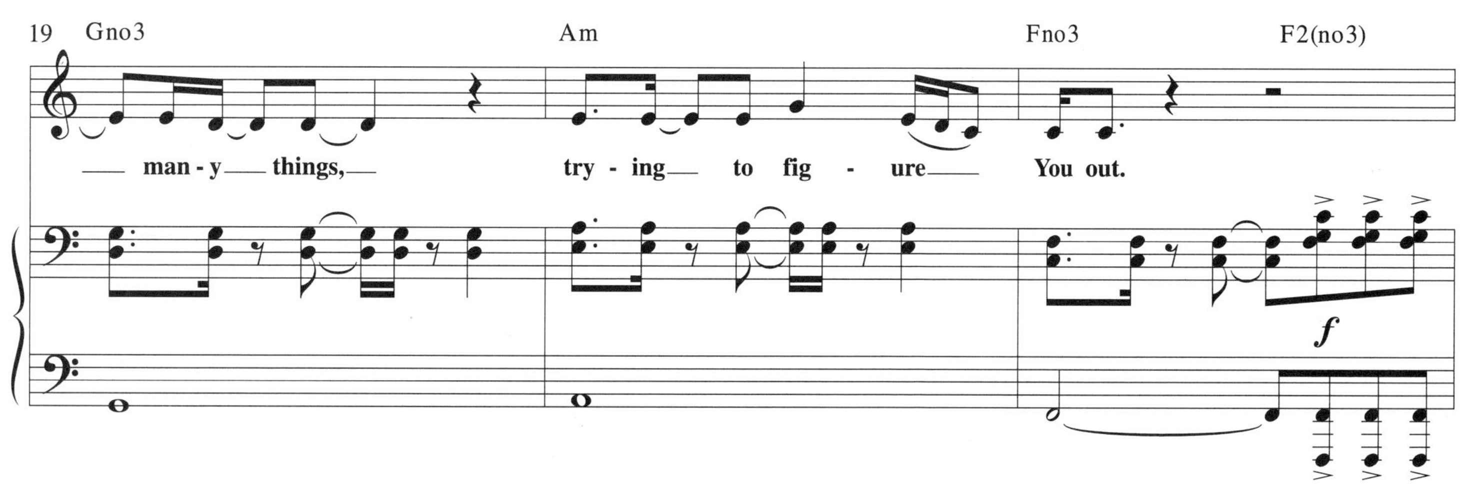
19 Gno3
Am
Fno3
F2(no3)
man - y things,
try - ing to fig - ure
You out.
f

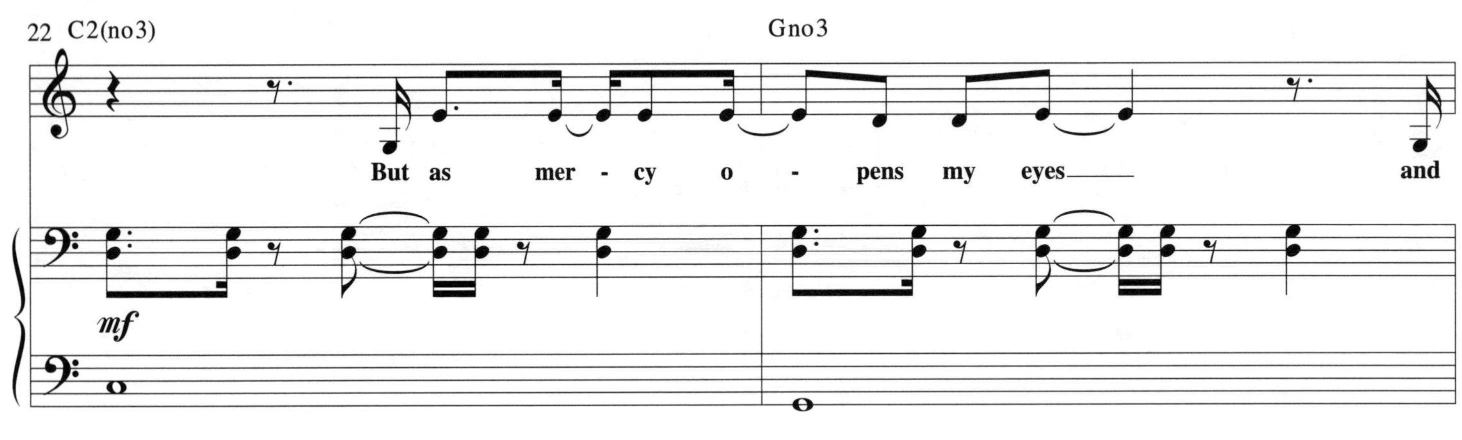
22 C2(no3)
Gno3
But as mer - cy o - pens my eyes and
mf

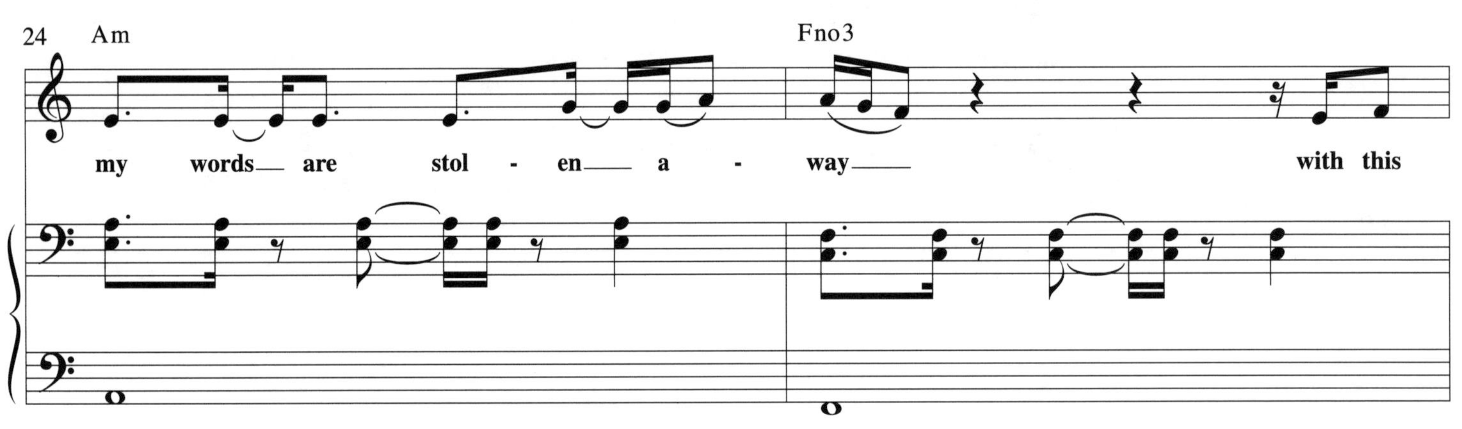
24 Am
Fno3
my words are stol - en a - way with this

26 Am
F2
f
breath - tak - ing view of Your grace. And I am
f

28 C
Dm7(4)
speech - less; I'm as - ton - ished and amazed. I am

30
Am7
F2(no3)
si - lenced by Your won - drous grace. You have
32
C
Am7
saved me; You have raised me from the
34
F2
F
G(add4)
F
F
F6
F
G
C
grave. And I am
36
C
Dm7(4)
speech - less in Your pres - ence now; I'm a -

38
Am7
F2(no3)
stound - ed as I con - si - der how You have
2nd time to CODA
40
Dm7
C2/E
F2(no3)
G7sus
shown us a love that leaves us
42
C
G
F2
F
G/F
F
G/F
F
G/F
speech - less.
44
C
G
F2
G/F
F

46 C2(no3)
mf
Gno3
2. So what kind of love could this be that would
mf
48 Am
Fno3
trade heav - en's throne for a cross?
50 C2(no3)
Gno3
And to think You still cel - e - brate o - ver
52 Am
Fno3
F2(no3)
find - ing just one who was lost.
f

54 C2(no3)
Gno3
And to know You re - joice o - ver us, the
mf
56 Am
Fno3
God of this whole u - ni - verse, it's a
58 Am
F2
D.S. al CODA 𝄋
f
sto - ry that's too great for words. And I am
f
CODA
60 Am7
Dm7 C/E F2 G(add4)
speech - less. We are

62
Dm/A
Am7
Dm7
C/E
F2
G(add4)
mf
speech - less.
Oh, how
64
F2
great is the love the Fa - ther has lav - ished up -
mf
66
Am9
on us,
that
68
Dm7(4)
C/E
F2
we should be called the sons and the daugh - ters of

70
B♭2
F/A
Dm7
Em7
F
G
Am7
G
God.
Yeah,
f
72
Fm7
Gm7
A♭
mf
B♭
C
G
C2(no3)
we are
speech - less.
We stand in awe of Your
mf
74
Dm7(4)
solo ad lib.
Am7
grace.
We stand in awe of Your
76
Fmaj7
G(add4)/F
C2(no3)
mer - cy.
We stand in awe of Your

78
Am7
Fmaj7
G(add4)/F
love.
We are
80
F
G(add4)/F
F
F6
f
F
G/C
C
speech - less.
We are
speech - less in Your
f
82
Dm7(4)
Am7
pres - ence now;
we're a - stound - ed as we con -
84
F2(no3)
Dm7
C2/E
si - der how
You have shown us a love that

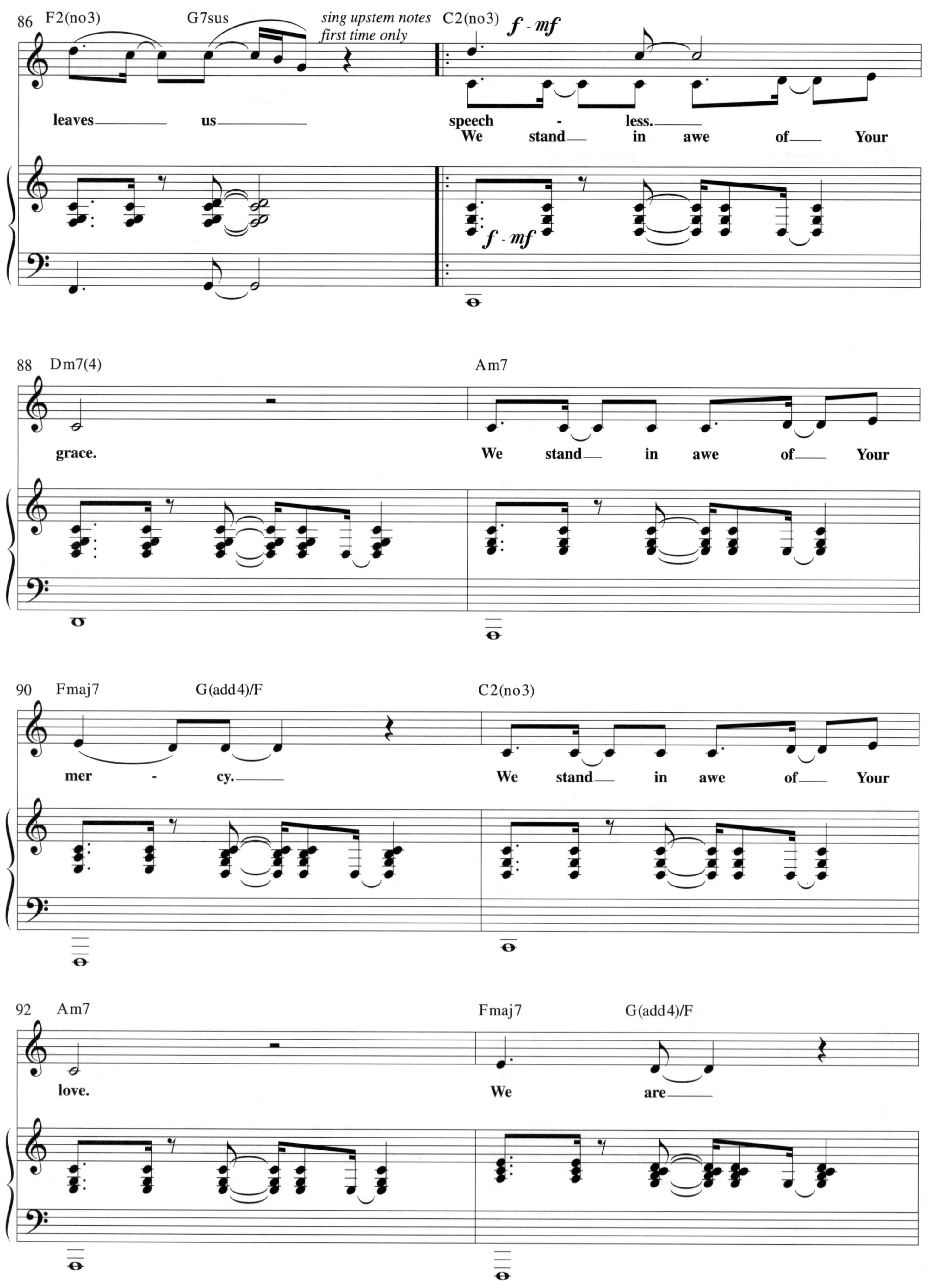
86
F2(no3)
G7sus
sing upstem notes first time only
C2(no3)
f - mf
leaves us
speech - less.
We stand in awe of Your
f - mf
88
Dm7(4)
Am7
grace.
We stand in awe of Your
90
Fmaj7
G(add4)/F
C2(no3)
mer - cy.
We stand in awe of Your
92
Am7
Fmaj7
G(add4)/F
love.
We are

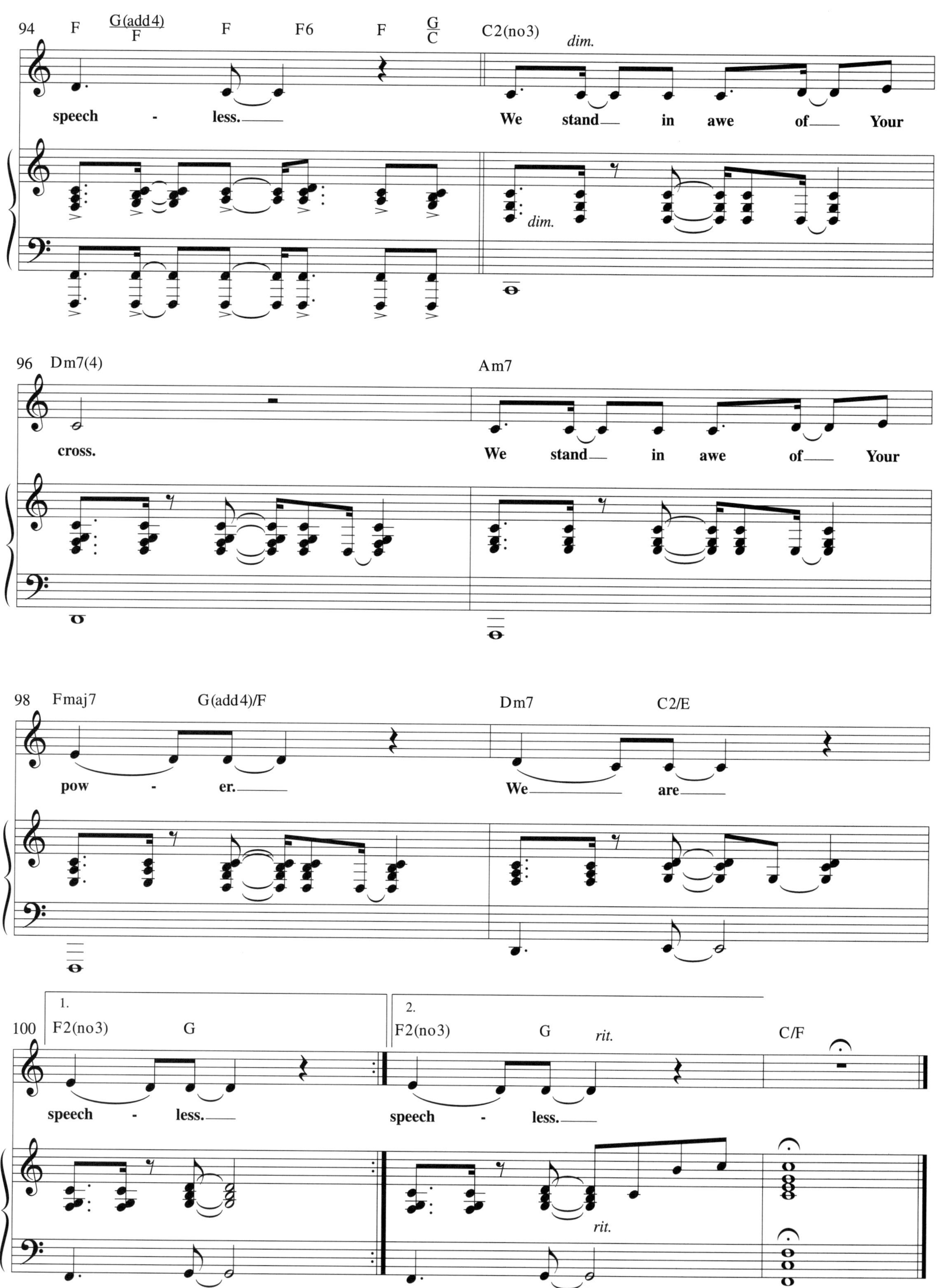
94
F
G(add4)/F
F
F6
F
G/C
C2(no3)
dim.
speech - less.
We stand in awe of Your
dim.
96
Dm7(4)
Am7
cross.
We stand in awe of Your
98
Fmaj7
G(add4)/F
Dm7
C2/E
pow - er.
We are
1.
2.
100
F2(no3)
G
F2(no3)
G
rit.
C/F
speech - less.
speech - less.
rit.

By Faith

Recorded by Michael Card

Words and Music by
MICHAEL CARD
and PHIL NAISH

15
A♭maj7
B♭
Cm(2)
- ly fear built an ark the world to save; an -
18
B♭
Fm9
B♭
oth - er left his home - land, and as a stran - ger he'd re - side.
21
A♭maj7
Cm
Cm/B♭
But none re - ceived the prom - ise then, and
24
A♭maj7
Fm
E♭/F
Fm
Fm
E♭/F
so, in faith, they died.

27
mf
Cm
Abmaj7
Bb
2. Oth - ers con - quered king - doms, quenched the fu - ry of the flames;
mf
30
Fm
Cm
Abmaj7
some made strong in bat - tle, some were
33
Bb
Cm(2)
Bb
raised to life a - gain. But man - y more were mar -
36
Fm9
Bb
Abmaj7
- tyred midst the crowds loud clam - or - ing. By

39
Cm
Cm/B♭
A♭maj7
faith, they would not bow the knee nor kiss the em - per - or's ring.
42
Fm
E♭/F
Fm
B♭
Faith un - der - stands and of -
45
Fm7
A♭
E♭
- fers, it as - sures and calms our fears; it can
48
B♭
Fm7
A♭
shut the mouths of li - ons and make sense of scars and tears.

51
B♭
A♭2
E♭/G
We per - se - vere in hope, and with con - science clean
54
G♭
A♭
B♭
and clear, we walk this fall - en wil -
57
Fm7
A♭
2nd time to CODA
A♭2
- der - ness with sal - va - tion's Pi - o - neer.
60
Cm7
A♭maj9
mf

63
mf
Cm
A♭maj7
3. Be - ing sure of what we hope for, see - ing
66
B♭
Fm
Cm
what is yet un - seen; a u - ni - verse from noth -
69
A♭maj7
B♭
Cm(2)
ing - ness, new life where none had been. The
72
B♭
Fm9
B♭
known made from un - know - a - ble, and hope for the com - fort - less

75
A♭maj7
Cm
Cm/B♭
who hear and hold on firm - ly to the
78
A♭maj7
Fm7
E♭/F
Fm
D.S. al CODA
faith that they pos - sess.
CODA
80
A♭2
B♭
mp
So
83
Fm
Cm
B♭
fix your eyes up - on the Cham - pi - on as you seek to run the
mp

86
A♭
Fm
Cm
race, un - der - stand - ing that He cheers you on
89
B♭
A♭2
G♭
as you long for His em - brace. So hold on and do not grow
92
D♭/F
F♭
C♭/E♭
wea - ry of the faith that you pro - fess, re -
95
D
A/C♯
Cm7
mem - ber - ing that you are ringed a - round by this cloud of wit - ness -

98
F
es.
f
B♭
Faith un - der - stands and of -
f
101
Fm7
- fers, it as - sures and calms our fears;
A♭
E♭
it can
104
B♭
shut the mouths of li - ons and make sense of scars and tears.
Fm7
A♭
107
B♭
A♭2
We per - se - vere in hope, and with con - science clean
E♭/G

110
G♭
A♭
B♭
and clear,
we walk this fall - en wil -
113
Fm7
A♭maj7
Fm
- der - ness
with sal - va - tion's Pi - o - neer.
116
B♭
Fm7
A♭
Faith un - der - stands and of - fers.
119
E♭
B♭
Fm7
Faith un - der - stands and of - fers.

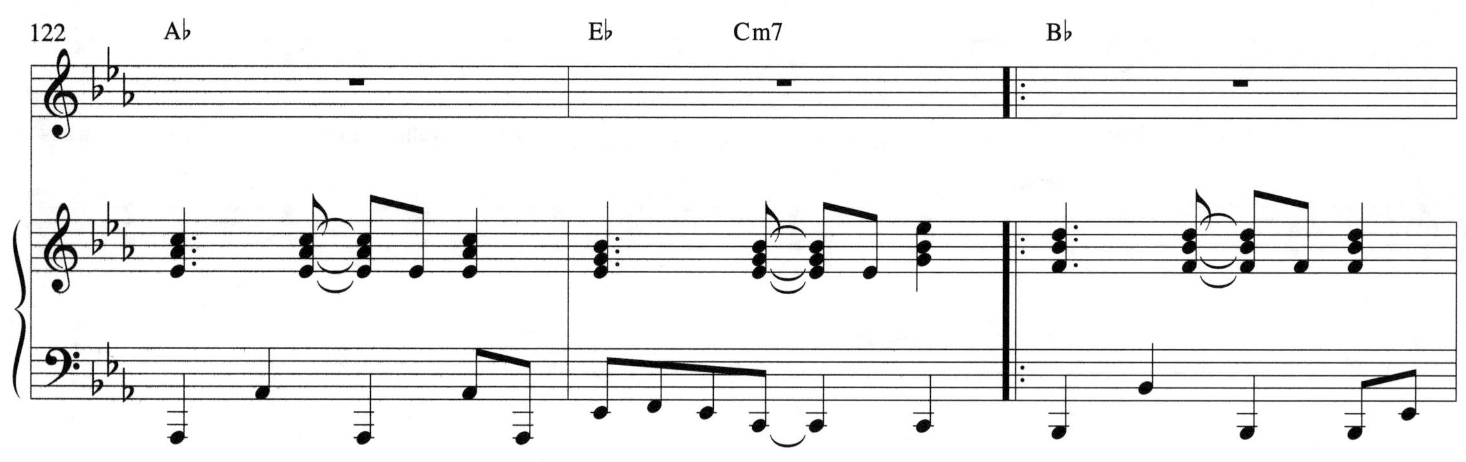
122
A♭
E♭
Cm7
B♭

125
Fm7
Repeat and Fade
A♭
E♭

128
Optional Song Ending
A♭
E♭

He Believes in You

Recorded by Aaron Benward

Words and Music by
AARON BENWARD, DARRELL BROWN
and DENNIS MATKOSKY

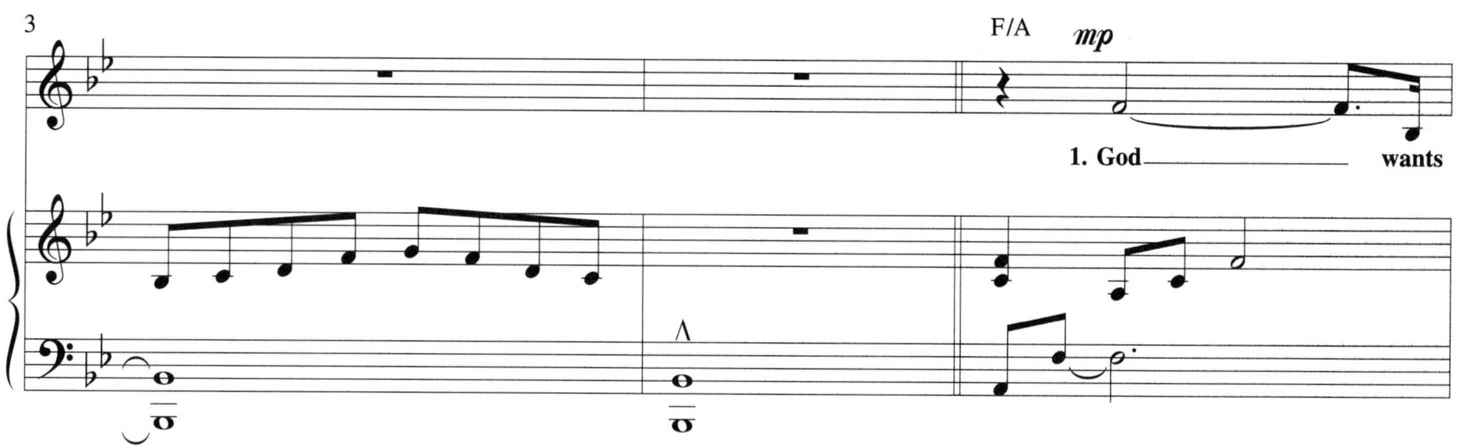

8
Gm2
F/A
heart.
Calm
10
E♭/G
B♭/F
all the whis - pers in your head,
just be still, lis - ten, you will
12
Gm2
Dm7
Gm
F
hear
ech - o - ing from deep in -
14
E♭maj9
B♭
F/A
mf
side:
He be - lieves in you
mf

16
Gm7
Gm7/F
E♭
B♭/D
and all the dreams you dream of.
Ev - 'ry hope and prayer you lean on,
18
E♭
Fsus
F
B♭
F/A
He will see them through.
And know that day is wait -
2nd time to CODA
20
Gm7
Gm7/F
E♭maj9
E♭
- ing just be - yond to - mor - row.
I know it's true; it's be -
22
Fsus
F
B♭sus
B♭
cause in you He be - lieves.

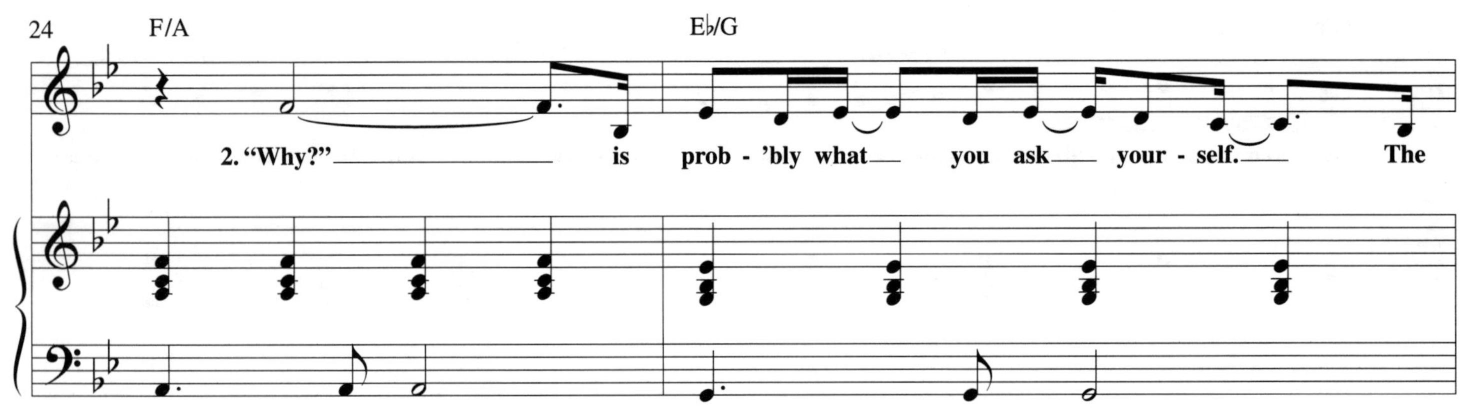
24
F/A
E♭/G
2. "Why?" is prob - 'bly what you ask your - self. The

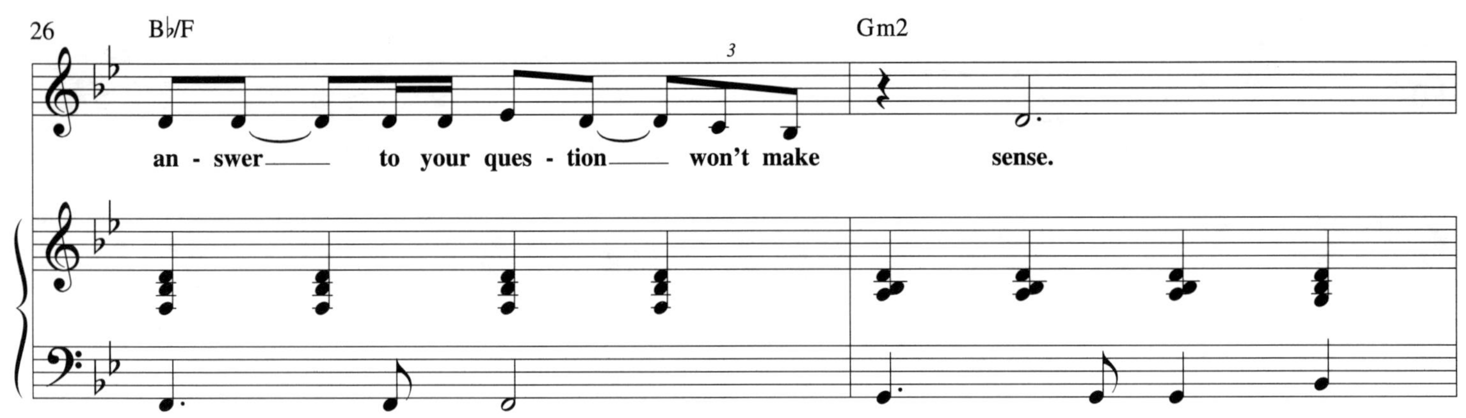
26
B♭/F
Gm2
3
an - swer to your ques - tion won't make sense.

28
F/A
E♭/G
God, He did - n't come to lift the proud, but

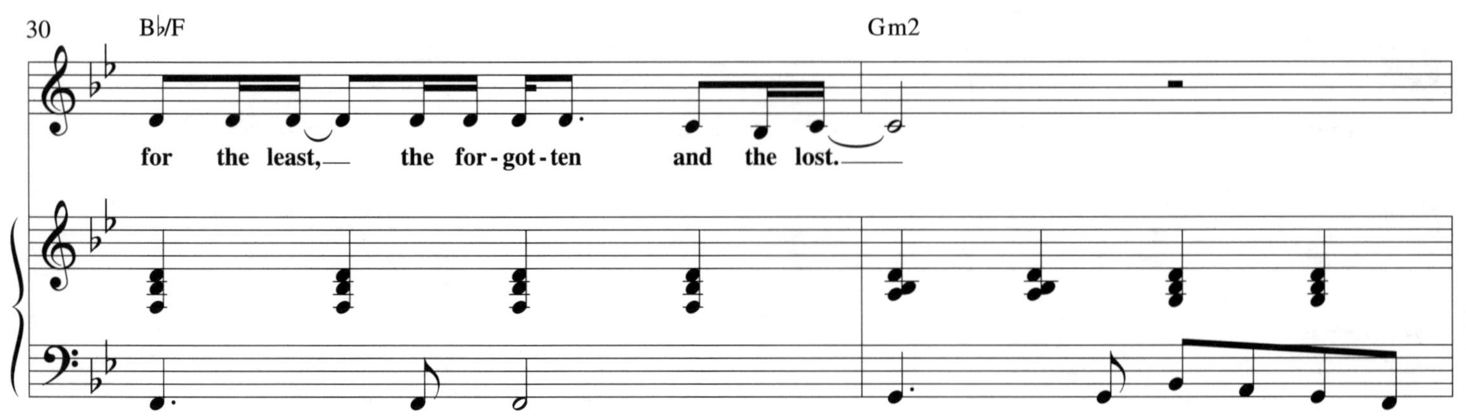
30
B♭/F
Gm2
for the least, the for-got-ten and the lost.

32
Dm7
Gm
F
E♭maj9
E - ven when it's hard to re - ceive, 'cause
34
Dm7
Gm
F
E♭maj9
D.S. al CODA
He made you for great - er things.
CODA
36
Fsus
F
E♭sus/A♭
cause in you, He be - lieves in you no mat - ter, no mat - ter
38
E♭/G
E♭sus/A♭
E♭/G
how you see your - self. Hold on to the un - chang - ing

40
B♭/F
F
heart, heart of God.
42
B
F♯/A♯
G♯m7
G♯m7/F♯
ff
He be - lieves in you and all the dreams you dream of.
ff
44
E
B/D♯
E
F♯sus
F♯
Ev - 'ry hope and prayer you lean on, He will see them through. And
46
B
F♯/A♯
G♯m7
G♯m7/F♯
know that day is wait - ing just be - yond to - mor - row.

48
Emaj7
C♯m/E
B/F♯
F♯
I know it's true; it's be - cause in you,
50
Emaj7
C♯m/E
C♯m9
C♯m7
I know it's true; it's be - cause in you
52
F♯sus
F♯
Emaj7
rit.
He be-lieves,
mf
rit.
54
F♯sus
mf
B
He be - lieves.

He's My Son

Recorded by Mark Schultz

Words and Music by
MARK SCHULTZ

16
Em
Bm
I'm hop - in' this prayer will turn out right.
19
A2/C♯
Em
See, there is a boy
22
Bm
A2/C♯
that needs Your help.
25
Em
Bm
A2/C♯
I've done all that I can do my - self.

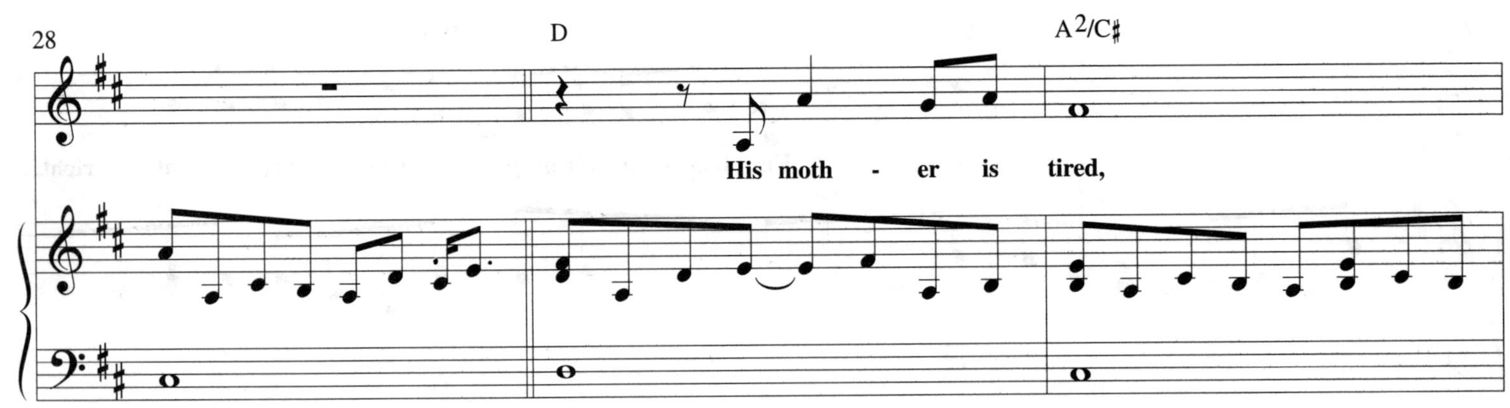
28
D
A2/C♯
His moth - er is tired,

31
Gmaj7/B
Asus
A
I'm sure You can un - der - stand.

33
D
A2/C♯
Gmaj7/B
Each night as he sleeps she goes in to hold

36
Asus
A
rit.
D/F♯
G2
D/F♯
G2
his hand, and she tries not to cry as the
rit.

39
D/F♯
G2
Asus
A
mf
tears fill her eyes. Can You
In tempo ♩ = 116
41
D/F♯
G2
Bm7(4)
hear me? Am I get - ting through to - night?
mf
44
Asus
D/F♯
G2
Can You see him? Can You make
47
Bm7(4)
Asus
D/F♯
him feel all right? If You can hear me

50
G2
Bm7(4)
Asus
let me take his place some - how. See, he's not
53
Em
D/F♯
G2
Asus
A
D/F♯
G
rit.
a tempo
just an - y - one, he's my son.
rit.
a tempo
2nd time to Coda
56
Bm7
Asus
A
D/F♯
G
Bm7
A
poco rit.
59
Em
Bm
A2/C♯
a tempo
mp
Some - times late at night I watch him sleep,

62
Em
Bm
I dream of the boy he'd like to be.

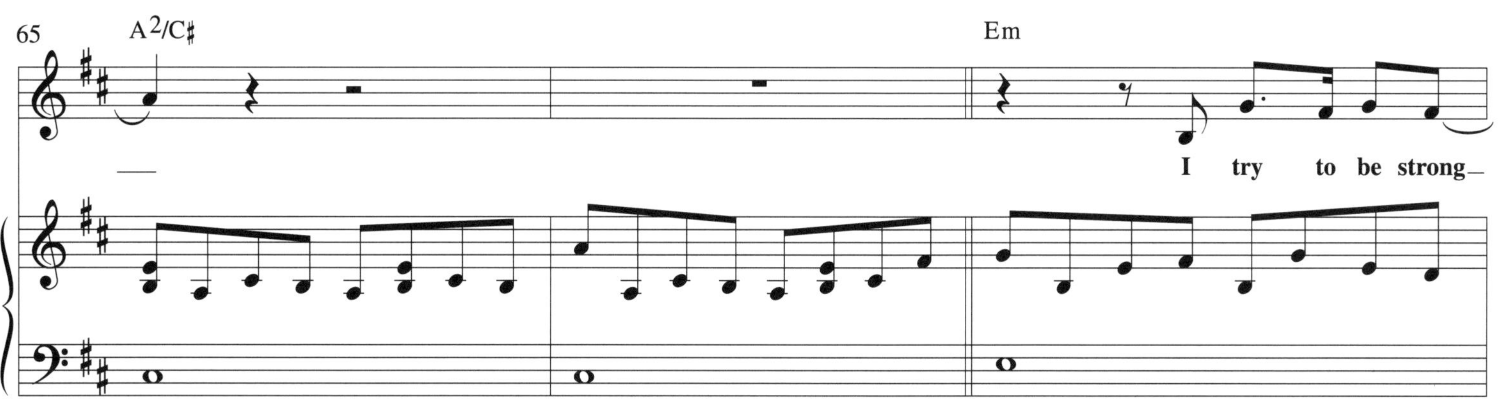
65
A2/C♯
Em
I try to be strong

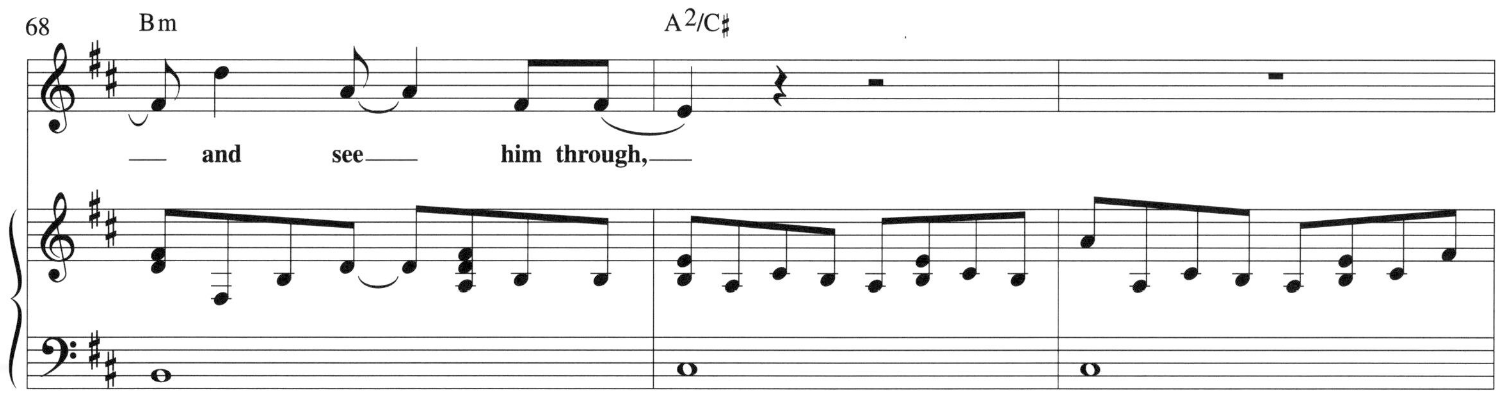
68
Bm
A2/C♯
and see him through,

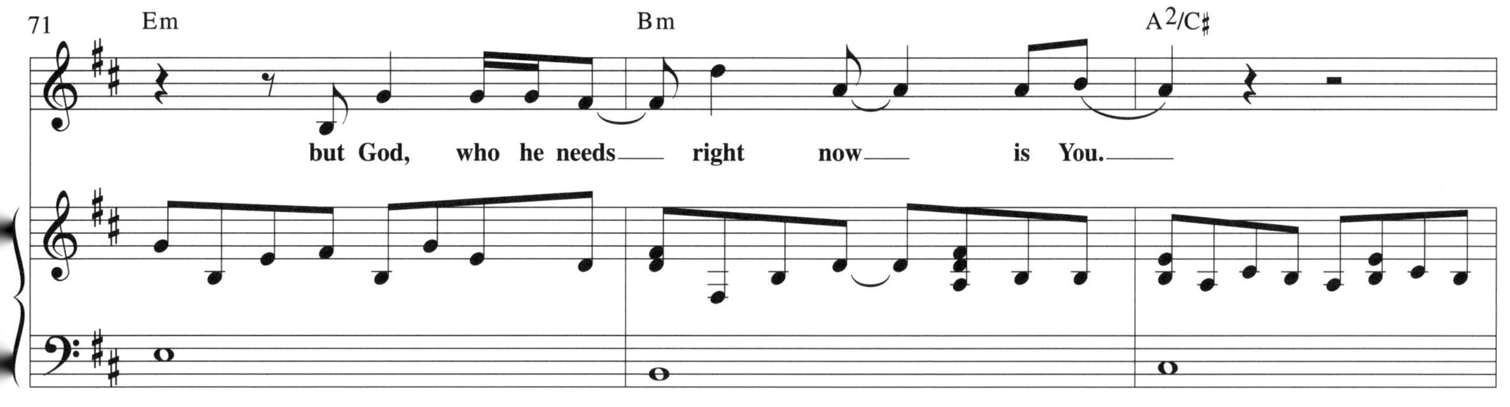
71
Em
Bm
A2/C♯
but God, who he needs right now is You.

74
D
A2/C♯
Gmaj7/B
Let him grow old,
live life with-out
78
Asus
A
D
A2/C♯
this fear.
What would I be
81
Gmaj7/B
Asus
A
D/F♯
G2
ten.
liv - ing with-out
him here?
He's so tired,
and he's
rit.
84
D/F♯
G2
D/F♯
G2
Asus
A
D.S. al CODA
rit.
scared,
let him know
that You're there.
Can You
rit.

CODA
87
D/F♯
a tempo
G
Bm7
Asus
A
a tempo
89
Em9
D2/F♯
G2
92
Asus
A
Em9
D2/F♯
95
G2
G2/B
rit.
Asus
A
f
Can You hear
rit.

97
D/F♯
a tempo
G2
Bm7(4)
me?
Am I get - ting through to - night?
f a tempo
100
Asus
D/F♯
G2
Can You see him?
Can You make
103
Bm7(4)
Asus
D/F♯
him feel all right?
If You can hear me
106
G2
Bm7(4)
Asus
let me take his place some - how.
See, he's not

109
Em
rit.
D/F♯
G2
mp
just an - y - one.
Can You hear
rit.
112
D/F♯
Slower, with rubato
G2
D/F♯
G2
me?
Can You see him?
Please don't
mp
Slower, with rubato
116
D/F♯
G2
Asus
D
a tempo
Em7
leave him,
he's my
son.
a tempo
120
D/F♯
G6
D
Em7
D/F♯
G6
rit.
D
rit.
pp
8vb

Cross of Christ

Recorded by Scott Krippayne

Words and Music by
SCOTT KRIPPAYNE
and DWIGHT LILES

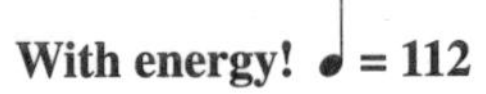

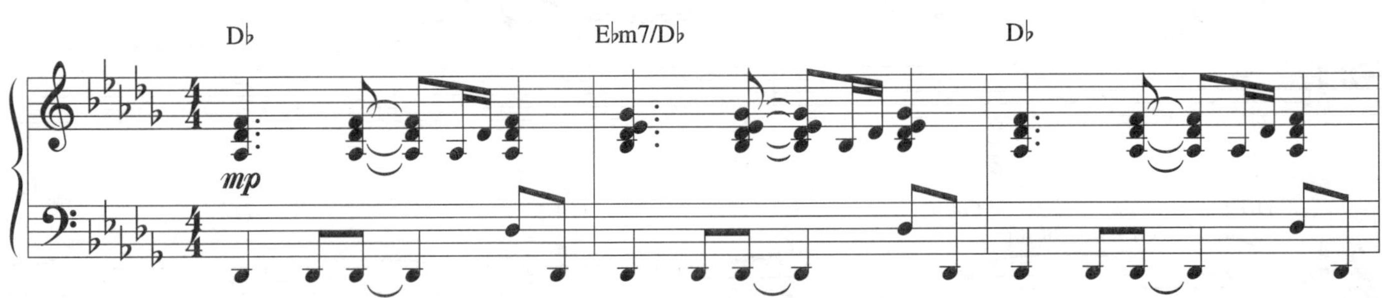

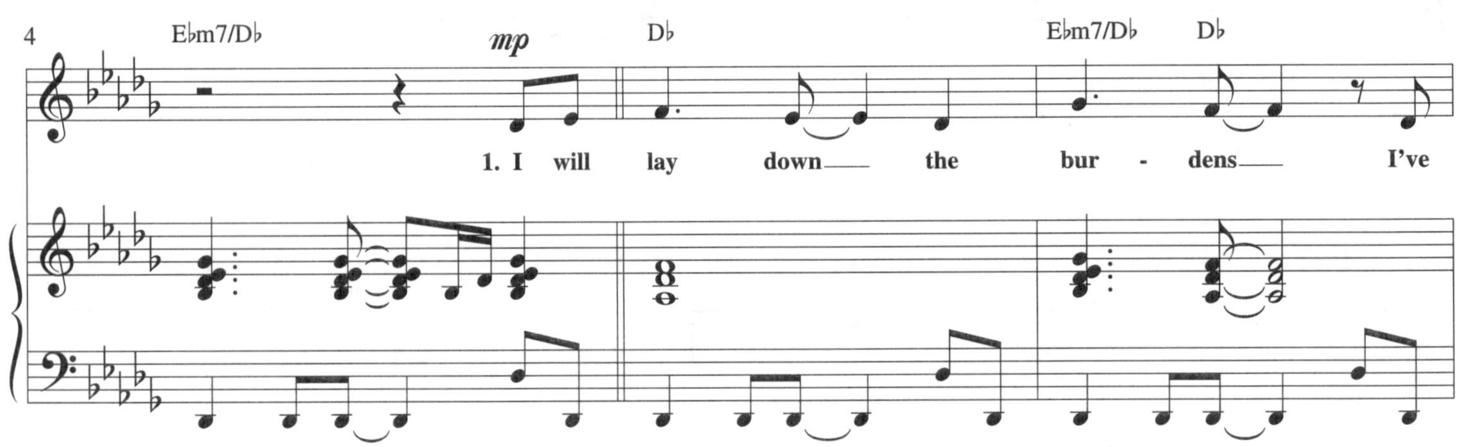

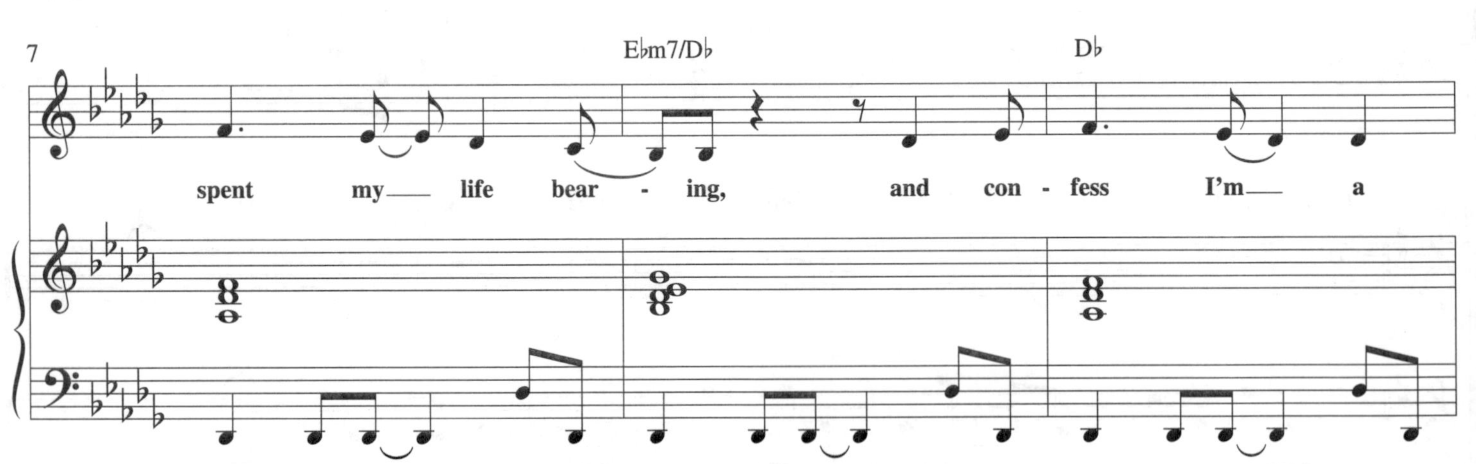

10
E♭m7/D♭
D♭
Fm7
sin - ner for whom Je - sus died. I will
13
G♭2(no3)
D♭2/F
D♭/G♭
live ev - 'ry mo - ment in the light of His mer -
16
D♭2/F
A♭7sus/E♭
D♭2/F
- cy, and I won't take for grant - ed His
19
D♭/G♭
D♭sus/G♭
D♭/G♭
A♭sus
A♭
mf
D♭
lov - ing sac - ri - fice. I will car - ry the cross of Christ,
mf

22
A♭sus A♭ G♭ G♭/D♭ D♭
hold to the hope I'm giv - en,
25
A♭7sus/E♭ D♭2/F G♭2(no3) A♭sus
(2nd time: ad lib.)
reach out to those in need and show them love, yeah, yeah.
28
G♭2/B♭ A♭/C D♭ A♭sus A♭
Yeah, with all of my soul and strength, as
cues 2nd time only
31
G♭ G♭/D♭ D♭ A♭7sus/E♭
long as my heart is beat - ing, I'll fol - low the One who laid

34
D♭2/F
G♭2(no3)
2nd time to CODA
A♭sus
down His life for mine and car - ry the cross of
37
D♭
Christ.
2. I will make it my
40
G♭/D♭
D♭
B♭m
A♭
G♭2(no3)
mis - sion to serve those a - round me, to
43
D♭
G♭/D♭
D♭
B♭m
care for the bro - ken and pray for the lost.

46
Fm7
A♭7sus/E♭
D♭2/F
I will walk in the foot - steps of my
49
D♭/G♭
B♭m9
A♭7sus/E♭
Lord and my Sav - ior, and I'll live out the gos -
52
D♭2/F
D♭/G♭
A♭sus
A♭
D.S. al CODA
- pel no mat - ter what the cost. I will
CODA
55
A♭sus
D♭
f
A♭/C
car - ry the cross of Christ. And I will

58
D♭
D♭/F
G♭2
E♭m7
not lay it down 'til I lay it at His feet.
f
61
D♭
A♭/C
D♭
D♭/F
G♭2
No, I will not lay it down 'til I touch
64
E♭m7
A♭sus
e - ter - ni - ty, yeah. I will
67
D♭
N.C.
A♭
G♭
car - ry the cross of Christ, hold to the hope I'm

70
G♭/D♭ D♭ A♭sus7/E♭ D♭2/F D♭/G♭
giv - en, reach out to those in need and show them love,
73
A♭sus G♭2/B♭ A♭/C D♭
show them love. Yeah, with all of my soul and strength,
76
A♭sus A♭ G♭ G♭/D♭ D♭
as long as my heart is beat - ing, I'll
79
A♭7sus/E♭ D♭2/F G♭2(no3)
fol - low the One who laid down His life for mine and

82
A♭sus
D♭
A♭sus
A♭
car - ry the cross of Christ. Hold
85
G♭
G♭/D♭
D♭
A♭7sus/E♭
to the hope I'm giv - en, reach out to those in need
88
D♭2/F
G♭2(no3)
A♭sus
G♭2/B♭
A♭/C
and show them love, show them love. Yeah, with
91
D♭
A♭sus
A♭
G♭
all of my soul and strength, as long as my heart is

94
G♭/D♭
D♭
A♭7sus/E♭
D♭2/F
beat - ing, I'll fol - low the One who laid down His life for
97
G♭2(no3)
E♭m7/A♭
mine and car - ry the cross of
99
D♭2(no3)
A♭2/C
Christ.
101
G♭2/B♭
G♭/A♭
D♭/A♭
E♭m/A♭
D♭/A♭

103
A♭7sus/E♭
E♭m7
D♭/E♭
Fm7
A♭sus/G♭
A♭sus
ad lib. to the end
106
G♭/B♭
A♭/C
D♭2
A♭(no3)
A♭sus
A♭
109
G♭2(no3)
G♭/D♭
D♭
D♭sus4/2
D♭
A♭sus7/E♭
112
D♭2/F
G♭2(no3)
A♭7sus
D♭

This Good Day

Recorded by Fernando Ortega

Words and Music by
FERNANDO ORTEGA and
JOHN ANDREW SCHREINER

11
B♭2(no3)
F
pour - ing down the hill;
fish - ing boats are leav - ing,
13
C
through my win - dow I can feel the o -
sea - gulls fol - low just a - bove the wa -
15
B♭2(no3)
- cean breeze.
- ter.
17
F
C
Nois - y spar - rows fill the oak trees,
I will wait un - til the sun - set

19 B♭2(no3)
F
swal - lows can't stay still; and
brings them home a - gain,
21
C
in the glad com - mo - tion, Lord, You speak
rig - ging lines and an - chors in the har -
23 B♭2(no3)
to me. If rain
- bor.
25 Dm Dm/E Dm/F G Gsus G Dm Dm/E Dm/F
clouds come or the cold winds blow,

28
G
Gsus
G
B♭2(no3)
C7/B♭
You're the one who goes be - fore me and
31
B♭2(no3)
C7/B♭
F
in my heart I know that this good day,
34
C/E
Gm7
B♭
it is a gift from You.
The world is turn -
37
F
C/E
Gm7
3rd time to CODA
- ing in its place be-cause You made it to.

40
B♭
E♭
B♭/D
I lift my voice to sing a song of praise
43
Csus
C
1.
F
on this good day.
46
C
B♭
F
49
2.
B♭2(no3)
B♭
F/A
Gm

52
Dm
D2(sus)
Dm
C/D
mf
55
G
Gsus
G
Dm
58
D2(sus)
Dm
C/D
G
Gsus
G
61
B♭
C/B♭
B♭
building
64
C/B♭
G
Am/G

67
G7
Am/G
D.S. al CODA 𝄋
f
If rain
CODA
69
B♭
F
C/E
This good day,
it is a gift
72
Gm7
B♭
F
from You.
The world is turn - ing in its place
75
C/E
Gm7
B♭
be-cause You made it to.
I lift my voice

78
E♭
Dm7
Csus
to sing a song of praise
81
C
F
C
on this good day.
84
B♭
F
87
C
B♭
F

Were It Not for Grace

Recorded by Larnelle Harris

Words and Music by
DAVID HAMILTON
and PHILL McHUGH

10
A♭
D♭maj7(♯4)
D♭maj7
In my soul I yearned to fol - low
12
C7sus
C7
F2(sus)
Fm
God but knew I'd nev - er be so
14
mf
E2
E
strong. I looked hard at this world to learn how
16
F♯
F♯2/A♯
F♯/A♯
B2(sus)/D♯
B/D♯
heav - en could be gained,

18
B2(sus)/D♯
B/D♯
E2
B/D♯
just to end where I be-gan, where hu - man
20
C♯sus
C♯m7/B
D♯sus/A♯
rit.
ef - fort is all in vain.
rit.
22
E♭/G
Cm7
D♭2
a tempo
D♭
E♭/D♭
Were it not for grace, I can tell you
a tempo
25
A♭
E♭/G
Fm7
B♭m
where I'd be: wan-d'ring down some point - less road to

28
E♭2(sus)
E♭/G
D♭/A♭
A♭
E♭/G
no - where, with my sal - va - tion up to
30
Fm
D♭
me. I know how that would go,
32
E♭/D♭
Cdim
Cm7(♭5)/F
F/A
F
the bat - tles I would face; for - ev - er
35
B♭sus
Bm
D♭/A♭
E♭
D♭/F
E♭/G
run - ning, but los - ing the race, were it not for

37
A♭sus
A♭
E♭/G Fm7
E♭
mp
D♭/E♭
grace.
2. So here is all my
mp
40
A♭
E♭
D♭2
A♭
E♭
praise,
ex - pressed with all my heart,
43
A♭
D♭maj7(♯4)
D♭maj7
C7sus
C7
of-fered to the Friend who took my place and ran a
46
Fsus
Fm
mf
E2
E
course I could not start. And when He saw in full just
mf

49
F♯sus
F♯/A♯
D♯m7
how much His love would cost,
51
E
He still went the fi - nal mile be - tween me and
53
C♯m7
E/B
D♯sus/A♯
rit.
hea - ven so I would not be lost.
rit.
55
E♭/G
D♭2
a tempo
E♭/D♭
Were it not for grace, I can tell you
a tempo

58
A♭ A♭2 E♭/G Fm7 B♭m
where I'd be: wan-d'ring down some point - less road to
61
B♭m7/E♭ E♭/G D♭/A♭ A♭ E♭/G
no-where, with my sal - va - tion up to
63
Fm D♭
me. I know how that would go,
65
E♭/D♭ E♭7/G Cm7(♭5)
the bat - tles I would face;

67
F7sus F F7/A
B♭m D♭/A♭
for - ev - er run - ning, but los - ing the
69
E♭/G D♭/F E♭/G Fm E♭ E♭/D♭ D♭2(no3) A♭/C
mp
race, were it not for grace. For - ev - er
mp
72
B♭m B♭m7/A♭ E♭ Fm E♭/G
run - ning, but los - ing the race, were it not for
74
A♭sus A♭
grace.
rit.

The Last to Be Chosen

Recorded by Ray Boltz

RAY BOLTZ

RAY BOLTZ and
STEVE MILLIKAN

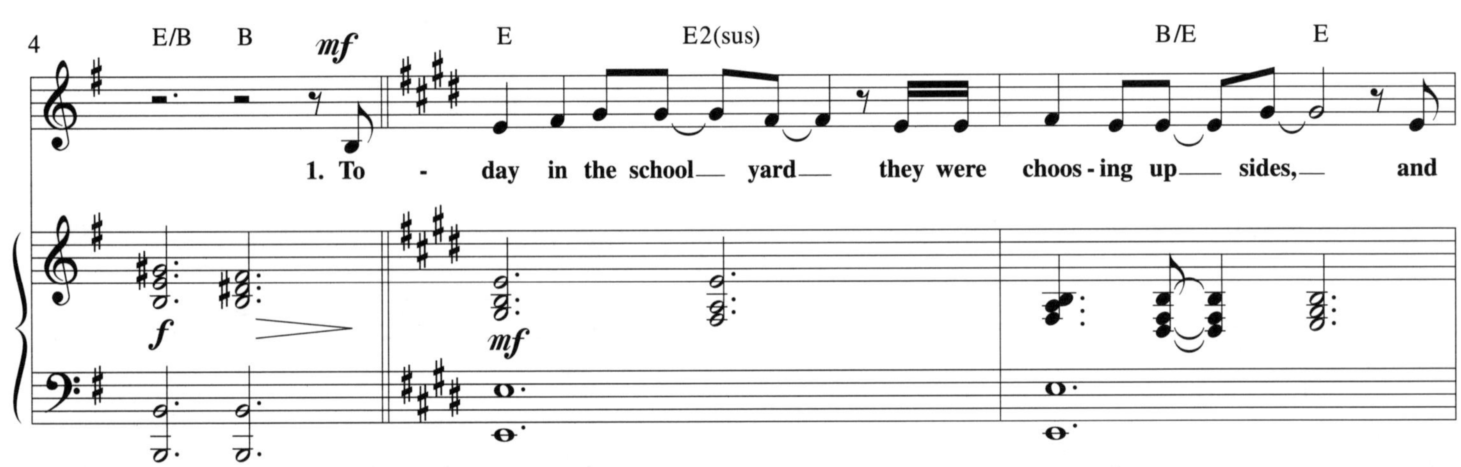

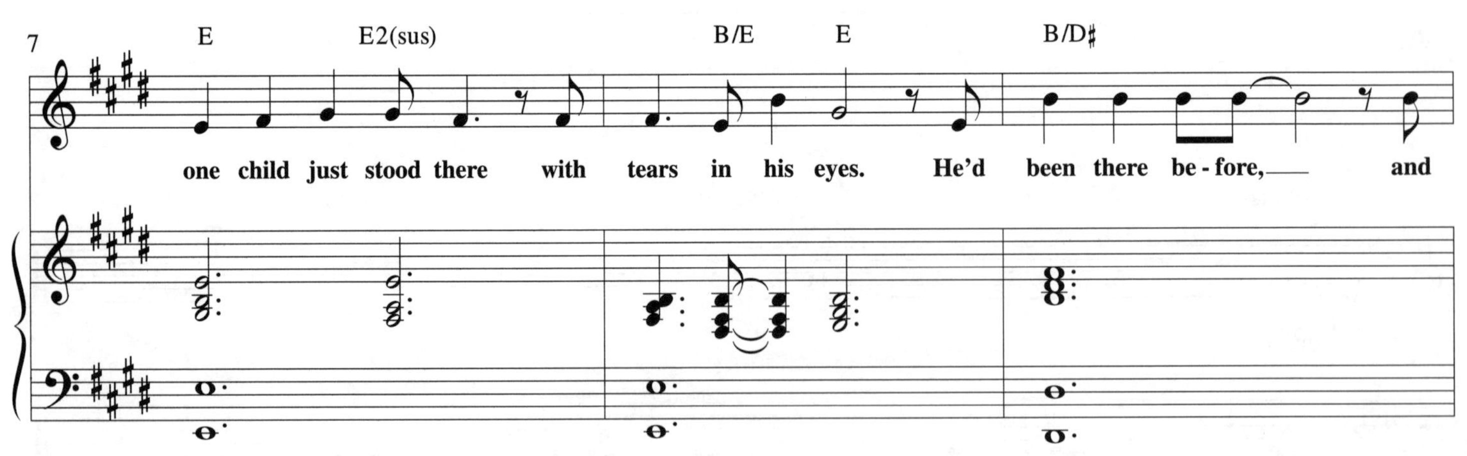

10
A2/C♯
E/B
A2(no3)
A
ev - 'ry - one knew he'd be a - lone when the choos - ing was
13
B
E
E2(sus)
through. 2. But high in the heav - ens the
(3.) don't be dis - cour - aged and
15
B/E
E
E2(sus)
Fa - ther looked down, and He saw what hap - pened
don't be a - fraid, God is not wor - ried with the
17
B/E
E
B/D♯
there on the ground. And an - gels re - joiced when He
choice that He made. Oth - ers may laugh or

19
A2/C♯
E/B
A
Bsus
B
f
said to His Son, "Watch what I do with this one." The
doubt at the start, but He sees what's there in your heart.
22
G
D/F♯
last to be chos - en are the first He will call. And
f
24
C/E
Dsus
D
what He does through them will a - maze one and all. It
26
G
Am7
G/B
C
D/C
won't be the he - ro that car - ries the ball,

29
C
C2(no3)
D7sus/A
G/B
the last to be chos - en are the
31
1.
C/E
D/F♯
C/E
G2/D
first He will call.
33
B♭
F2/A
D2/F♯
8va
E/B
B
mf
3. Now
f
36
2.
C/E
D/F♯
G/B
C/E
first He will call.

38
A/C♯
G♯m7
D/F♯
G♯m/D♯
D♭/F
ff
The
41
G♭
D♭/F
last to be chos - en are the first He will call.
And
ff
43
C♭/E♭
D♭sus
D♭
what He does through them will a - maze one and all.
45
G♭
A♭m7
G♭/B♭
C♭
D♭/C♭
Stand - ing for Je - sus when oth - ers may fall,

48
C♭
A♭m7
G♭/B♭
the last to be chos - en are the
50
C♭/E♭
D♭/F
G♭
D♭/G♭
G♭
first He will call.
52
C♭/E♭
D♭
C♭
C♭/E♭
D♭/F
G♭
The last to be chos - en are the
54
D♭/F
C♭/E♭
first He will call.
And what He does through them will a -

56
Gb/Db
Dbsus
Db
Gb
Abm7
maze one and all.
Stand-ing for Je-sus when
59
Gb/Bb
Cb
Db/Cb
Cb
oth-ers may fall,
the
62
Abm7
Gb/Bb
Cb/Eb
Db/F
last to be chos-en are the first
He will
64
Cb/Eb
Gb2/Db
A
E2/G♯
Dbno3 Fbno3 Gb2(no3)
slower
call.
f
slower

Morning Star

Recorded by Steve Green

Words and Music by
MICHAEL CARD

14
B♭
C
Dm
Gm7
Morn - ing Star, oh Morn - ing Star; and I must cross it be -
17
C/D
Dm
B♭
C
fore the night, Bright and Morn - ing Star.
20
Gm7
C/D
Dm
2. The day can be too much for me,
23
B♭
C
Dm
Gm7
Morn - ing Star, oh Morn - ing Star; be Thou my vi - sion so

26
C/D
Dm
B♭
C
I can see,
Bright and Morn - ing Star,
29
B♭
F
Bright and Morn - ing Star.
Come
32
B♭/F
F
C
rise and shine in Your ho - li -
35
F
B♭
F
ness, oh, ra - diant Son of

38
C
Dm
Gm7
Right - eous - ness; and warm Your
41
F
C
Dm
peo - ple both near and far, and
44
B♭
F
C
F
B♭
2nd time to CODA
shine through me, oh, Morn - ing Star, shine through me, oh,
47
C
Gm7
C/D
Dm
Morn - ing Star.

50
B♭
Gm7
C/D
Dm
54
B♭
mf
Gm7
3. Now like a bea - con
mf
57
C/D
Dm
B♭
C
Dm
come and blaze, Morn - ing Star, oh Morn - ing Star; lead
60
Gm7
C/D
Dm
B♭
on, Good Shep - herd, through the maze, Bright and Morn - ing Star,

D.S. al CODA
63
C
B♭
F
f
Bright and Morn - ing Star. Come
CODA
66
C
Dm
Morn - ing Star. Your com-pas -
69
B♭
C
Dm
- sion's new ev - 'ry morn - ing;
72
Gm7
C
it fills us up so we can sing,

75
Dm
Gm7
78
C
Dm
so we can sing.
81
Gm7
C
Oh, come
84
B♭/F
F
C
rise and shine in Your ho - li -

87
F
B♭
F
ness, oh, ra - diant Son of
90
C
Dm
Gm7
Right - eous - ness; and warm Your
93
F
C
Dm
C/D
Dm
peo - ple both near and far,
96
B♭
F
C
F
and shine through me, oh, Morn - ing Star,

99
B♭
C
Gm7
ad lib. on repeats
shine through me, oh, Morn - ing Star.
102
C/D
Dm
B♭
Morn - ing Star, oh, Morn - ing Star.
105
Gm7
C/D
Dm
Repeat ad lib.
B♭
Shine through me, oh,
108
C
Final ending
B♭
Dm
C
B♭
Morn - ing Shine through me, oh, Morn - ing Star.

Living Water

Recorded by Bob Carlisle

Words and Music by
RANDY THOMAS and
BOB CARLISLE

In a strong four ♩ = 84

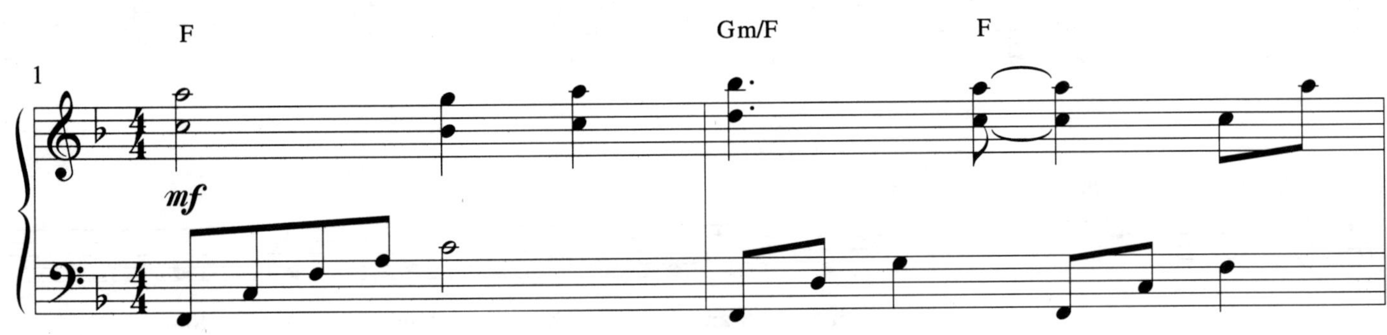

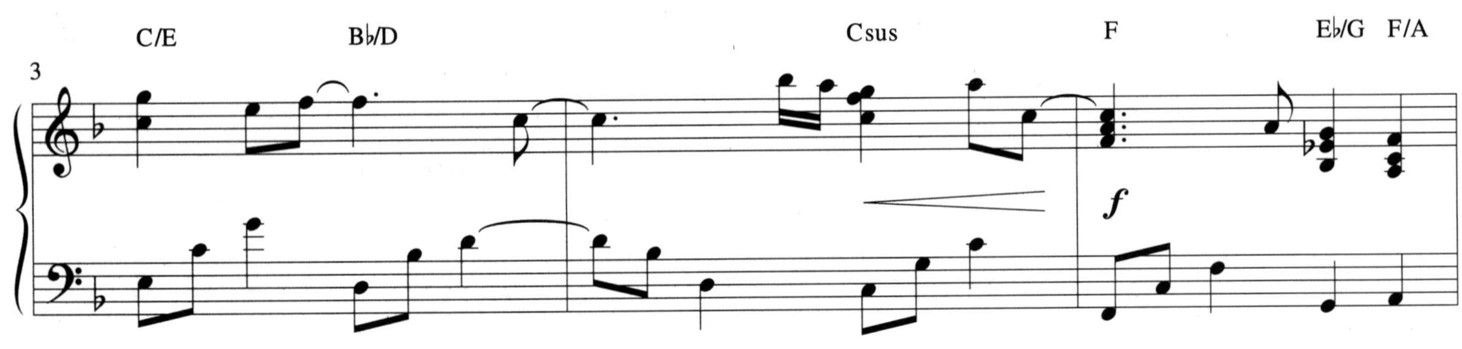

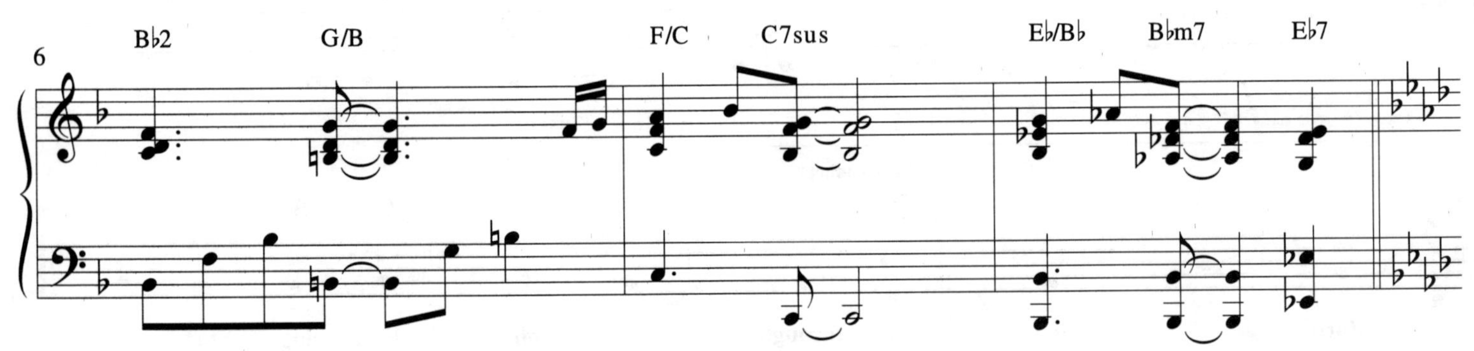

9
A♭
mf
E♭2/G
1. I feel Your touch, I can feel Your heart as I'm
2. Lord, so man - y times You've called my name and I've
mf
11
D♭2/F
A♭/E♭
E♭
ly - ing here a - lone in the dark.
turned my face the oth - er way.
13
A♭
E♭2/G
B♭2/D
I hear Your voice gent - ly say, "Come to
Yet, be - fore I e - ven saw the womb, You loved
16
C/E
Fm
E♭/F
A♭/C
Me." I long for Your love
me. How could I be so blind,

18
D♭
A♭/E♭
Like the earth longs for the
when I a - lone have cre - at - ed my
20
D♭maj7
A♭/E♭
rain - fall. I'm wea - ry, Lord, I've
dark - ness? For - give me, and
22
D♭/E♭
E♭7/G
A♭
D♭2/E♭
C7sus
C7
f
wan - dered this des - ert too long.
wash me clean a - gain.
So
25
F
Gm/F
F
Gm/F
F
C2/E
B♭2/D
come, Liv - ing Wa - ter, flow through me like a
f

28
F/C
C7sus
C7
F
Gm/F
F
Gm/F
F
riv - er.
My heart's been thirst - ing so
31
Gsus
G/B
Gm/C
C/B♭
F/A
long.
Flood through my
34
B♭maj7
B♭6
F/C
A7/C♯
Dm7
G2
G
soul and pour out Your mer - cy.
37
F/C
Gm/C
F/C
Gm/C
C7sus
1.
D♭2
E♭2
E♭
Come, Liv - ing Wa - ter, fill me.

41
2.
F
B♭/F
F
Fm
ff
A♭
B♭m/A♭
A♭
me.
Come, Liv - ing
ff
44
B♭m/A♭
A♭
E♭2/G
D♭2/F
A♭/E♭
E♭7sus
Wa - ter, flow through me like a riv - er.
47
A♭
B♭m/A♭
A♭
B♭m/A♭
A♭
B♭sus
B♭
My heart's been thirst - ing so long.
50
E♭7sus
E♭7/D♭
A♭/C
D♭
Flood through my soul and

53
A♭/E♭
C7/E
Fm
B♭9sus
B♭9
A♭/E♭
B♭m/E♭
A♭/E♭
pour out Your mer - cy.
Come, Liv - ing
56
B♭m/E♭
C/E
Fm
Fm7
B♭9sus
B♭7
Wa - ter, fill me.
59
A♭/E♭
B♭m/E♭
A♭/E♭
B♭m/E♭
F♭2
F♭
mf
rit.
Come, Liv - ing Wa - ter, fill me.
62
B♭m7(♭5)/D♭
B♭m7(♭5)
A♭2

Never Be

Recorded by Carman

Words and Music by
CARMAN

9
F/C
C7sus
C2/E
nev - er be a time that He would ev - er turn His back on me,
3
11
D2/F♯
Gm7
B♭m6/D♭
C7sus
there'll nev - er be a life He can't re - store.
13
F
Gm/B♭
F
Gm/B♭
15
F
B♭/F
B♭m6/D♭
mf
B♭/C
F/G
Gm
F/G
Gm
Where do you go when you feel like

17
Em11
B♭maj9
you've been for - sak - en,
pure - ly for - got - ten,
all a - lone?
19
Fmaj9
F/G
Gm
F/G
Gm
What do you do when your dreams have been
21
Em11
B♭maj9
bro - ken and shat - tered;
does it real - ly mat - ter
to an - y -
23
Fmaj9
Cm/A
D7(♭9)
one?
There is a Man
stand - ing with arms o - pen

25
Gm7
B♭m6
Am7
A♭13
wide, dry - ing the tears that I've cried, lov - ing me and giv - ing
27
Gm7(4)
B♭/C
C
life. And there'll
29
F
B♭2/F
C/F
F
A7
nev - er be a heart that He could - n't mend each bro - ken piece,
31
Dm7
G13
G7
C7sus
B♭m6/D♭
C7sus
nev - er be a wound - ed soul He would ig - nore. And there'll

33
F
B♭/F
C
C/E
nev - er be a time that He would ev - er turn His back on me,
35
D/F♯
Gm
B♭m6/D♭
C7
there'll nev - er be a life He can't re - store.
37
F
f
Emaj7
Am6/B
And nev - er will I doubt a - gain,
f
39
E
Am
Emaj7
Am6/B
3
I will nev - er be with - out a friend, nev - er will my eyes fail to see what the

41
B♭
D7sus
rit.
E♭7sus
D♭/E♭
E♭
Lord did for me. And there'll
rit.
43
A♭
D♭
E♭/G
A♭
B♭m7
A♭/G♭
C7/E
a tempo
nev-er be a heart that He couldn't mend each bro-ken piece, I know there'll
a tempo
45
Fm
B♭9
B♭m7
F♭/G♭
G♭
molto rit.
nev-er be a wound-ed soul He would ig-nore. And there'll
molto rit.
47
C♭maj7
F♭maj7
G♭/B♭
Broader
nev-er be a time that He would ev-er turn His back on me,
Broader

49
A♭/C
B♭m7
there'll
nev - er be,
no, there'll
51
G♭9 sus
B♭m7
nev - er be,
nev - er be
53
D♭/E♭
mf
A♭
D♭/A♭
B♭m/A♭
a life He can't re - store.
mf
55
A♭
D♭/A♭
B♭m/A♭
A♭/E♭
D♭/E♭
D♭m(♯7)/F♭
E♭7sus
A♭
molto rit.
molto rit.

Smellin' Coffee

Recorded by Chris Rice

Words and Music by
CHRIS RICE

Easy groove ♩ = 112

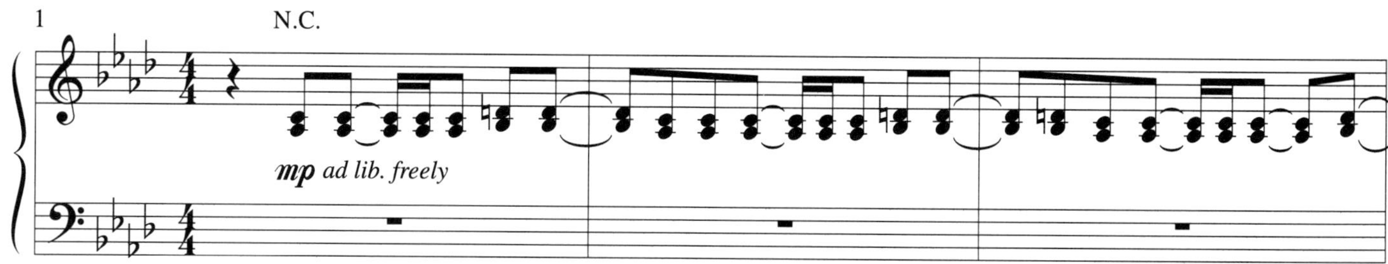

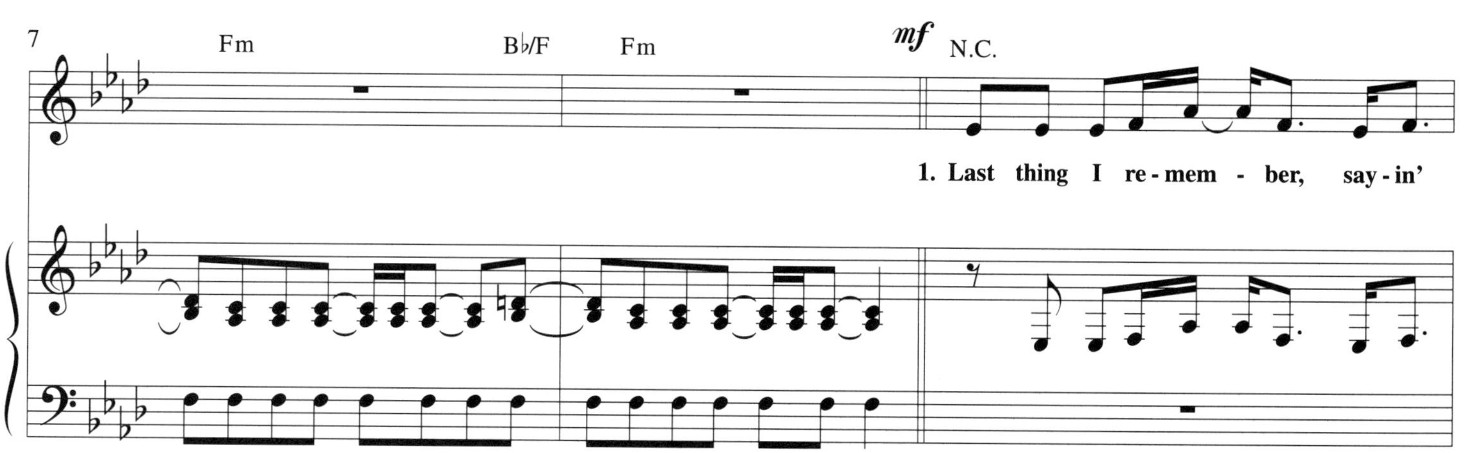

10
bye to yes - ter - day.
Glad to see it o - ver, pull - in'
12
cov - ers o - ver my head.
But what were You do - in' while I
14
dreamt the night a - way?
'Cause I can
C7
tell that some - thin's dif - f'rent and my
16
B♭7
eyes ain't e - ven o - pen yet.
f
F7
cue 2nd time only
B♭7
I'm smell - in' cof - fee, birds
f

18
E♭
B♭m7
F7
B♭7
are sing-in' just out - side. Here comes Your mer - cy stream -
20
E♭
B♭m7
F7
B♭7
- in' in with the morn - ing light. My heart is rac - ing wak -
2nd time to CODA
22
E♭
B♭m7
B♭/F
F7
B♭7
- ing up to Your smile, it's a good morn - ing,
2nd time: (say - in')
24
B♭/F
F7
yeah, it's a good morn-ing. 2. Well,

27
B♭7
I re-mem - ber read - in' You're the God___ who nev - er___ sleeps.
29
F7
B♭7
And while I've been dream - in', You've been sing - ing o - ver me,___ yeah.
31
F7
B♭7
Sing-in' a-bout___ my free - dom, wak-in' me up___ to hear___ Your song,___ and now I
D.S. al CODA
33
C7
B♭2(no3)/E♭
can't___ dance hard e-nough,___ 'cause yes - ter-day___ is gone, gone,___ gone!___

CODA
35
F7
B♭7/F
good morn - ing, yeah, yeah, yeah,
37
F7
B♭/F
good morn - ing, yeah.
39
B♭ B♭2 B♭(no3)
Am7 D Am7 D
Drum fill
Ooo, Ooo,
42
Am7 D A♭m7 D♭ A♭m7 D♭
Ooo. Ooo, Ooo,

45
A♭m7
D♭
F7
Ooo.
3. Ev - 'ry lit - tle breath, ev - 'ry heart - beat is a
47
B♭7
F7
gift of love that You give to me. You keep giv - in', e - ven when I'm a - sleep, 'cause I
49
B♭7
F7
know You nev - er stop watch - ing o - ver me. I wake up, my past is gone, 'cause Your
51
B♭7
F7
mer - cy's new with the morn - in' sun. I'm for - giv - en, I'm free, it's a brand new day, 'cause Your

53
B♭7
F7
B♭7
faith - ful - ness is the great - est! Hey! I'm smell - in' cof - fee, birds
55
E♭
B♭m7
F7
B♭7
are sing - in' just out - side. Here comes Your mer - cy stream -
57
E♭
B♭m7
F7
B♭7
- in' in with the morn - ing light. My heart is rac - ing wak -
59
E♭
B♭m7
F7
B♭7
- ing up to Your smile. I'm smell - in' cof - fee, birds

61
E♭
B♭m7
F7
B♭7
— are sing-in' just out - side. Here comes Your— mer - cy stream -
63
E♭
B♭m7
F7
B♭7
- in' in— with the morn - ing light. My heart is rac - ing wak -
65
E♭
B♭m7
F7sus
ad lib. on repeats
F7
- ing up— to Your smile,— say - in' good morn - ing,
ad lib. on repeats
67
B♭/F
F7sus
F7
yeah,— yeah, yeah. It's a good morn - ing,—

69
B♭/F
Repeat 3 times
B♭/F
F
B♭/F
oh.

71
F
B♭/F

73
1.
2.
B♭7/F

Merciful Heaven

Recorded by Wayne Watson

Words and Music by
WAYNE WATSON

Gospel feel ♩ = 72

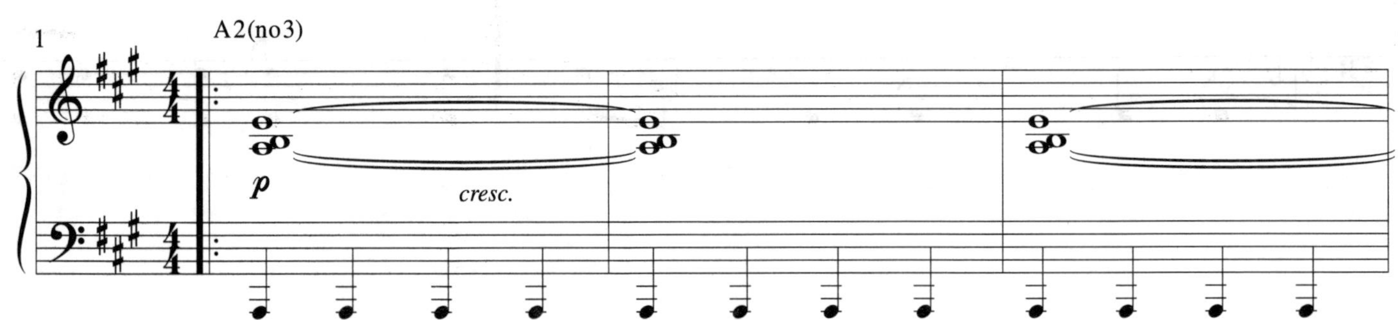

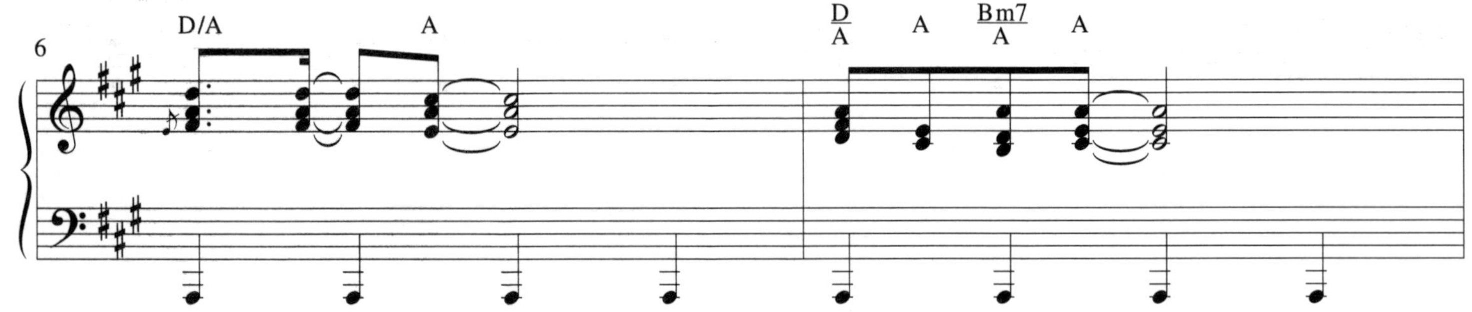

10
D
A
Bm9
12
D/E
A
A
mf
E
Mer - ci - ful Heav - en, have
14
D
A
D
A
mer - cy on me;
sev - en times sev - en,
16
D
E
A
E
I've al - ways be - lieved.
You've got the pow - er and

3rd time to CODA
D
A
Bm2
I have the need;
Mer - ci - ful Heav - en have
D/E
A
mer - cy on me.
1. Some peo - ple want what they de - serve,
2. This is a place where I can live:
D2
F♯m
C♯m/E
but not me, no, I know my heart too well.
at Your feet for - giv - en per - fect - ly.
D2
A
And I've just bare - ly got the nerve
'Cause I've got noth - ing good to give,

26
E/D D F♯m F♯m/E E
just to make this one re - quest, and I know
noth - ing more than just my - self. I know You
28
1.
D Esus E
that You will hear me.
2.
D.S. al CODA
D Esus E
want for noth - ing else.
CODA
30
D/E A F♯/A♯ Bm
mer - cy on me.
mp
32
E/G♯ A D/F♯ G D/F♯

34
C♯/E♯
F♯/A♯
Bm
mf
36
E/G♯
A
D/F♯
G
D/F♯
38
Bm
D/E
A
E
Mer - ci - ful Heav - en, have
cresc.
f
40
D2
A
D
A
mer - cy on me;
sev - en times sev - en, I've
42
Bm7
E
A
E
al - ways be - lieved that You've got the pow - er and

44
D2
A
Bm7
I have the need;
Mer - ci - ful Heav - en, have
46
D/E
A
Bm7
mer - cy on me.
Mer - ci - ful Heav - en,
48
D/E
A
E
have mer - cy on me.
mf
50
D
A
Bm9
D/E
A

I Will Follow Christ

Recorded by Clay Crosse featuring BeBe Winans and Bob Carlisle

Words and Music by
CLAY CROSSE
and STEVE SILER

With conviction! 𝅗𝅥 = 72

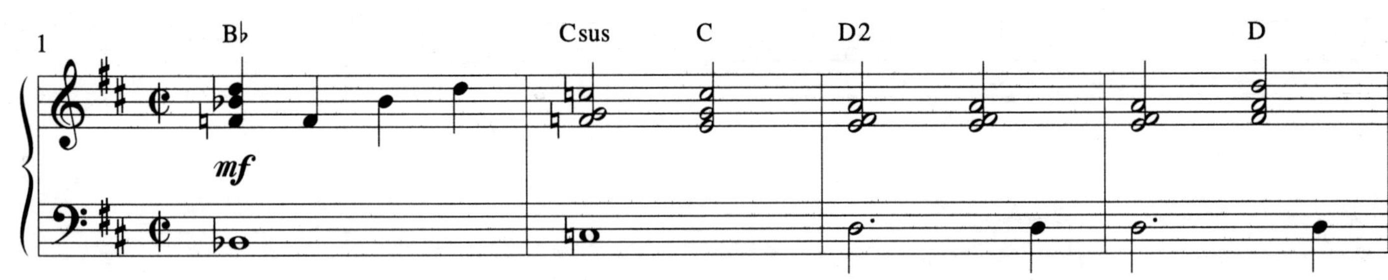

12
Gm7
F2/A
B♭
the Fa - ther was a broth - er to you all.
there were times you did - n't un - der - stand.
16
F2/A
Gm7
The teach - ing that we heard
When He had to go
19
Dm
B♭
was the Liv - ing Word; the won - ders and the mir -
and you felt a - lone, must have been so hard
22
A7sus
1.
A7
2.
A7
- a - cles you saw.
to see His plan.
I

26
B♭
Csus
C
Am7
think a - bout the way you car - ried on.
29
B♭
Gm7
3
in the face of per - se - cu - tion, you stand
32
A7sus
A7sus
A/C♯
mf
D
D/F♯
strong. So I will fol - low Christ, I will run the
36
A
D/F♯
race, fight - ing the good fight, stand - ing on my

40
G
f
E7/G♯
faith. I will wear the name of Je - sus, I will
f
44
D/A
Bm7
Em7
give Him all my life. As for me, no mat - ter what
47
D/F♯
2nd time to CODA
B♭
Csus
C
D
the sac - ri - fice, I will fol - low Christ.
51
mf
B♭
3. Now I don't have to look
mf

55
Csus
C
D2
Gm7
a - cross the a - ges.
His voice is speak - ing in
59
F2/A
B♭
F2/A
Gm7
my heart to - day.
His word is like a flame
63
Dm
con - sum - ing all my shame;
His
66
B♭
A7sus
A7
D.S. al CODA 𝄋
life, a shin - ing star to show the way.
Yes, I will fol - low

CODA
70
B♭
Csus
C
F
Yes, I will fol - low Christ. I be - hold
73
C/E
(cue optional)
Cm/E♭
Your life and see the man You want me to be - come.
simile
77
D7sus
D7
B♭m6/D♭
Oh, liv - ing like some - one whose heart be - longs to the
81
F/C
3
king - dom that was sealed on Cal - va - ry.

84
Gm7
Asus
A
I will show the world what I be - lieve.
I will fol - low,
88
ff
E
(cue optional)
B
B/A
I will, I will run the race,
fight - ing the good fight,
ff
92
E/G♯
A
stand - ing on my faith.
I will
96
F♯7/A♯
E/G♯
C♯m
wear the name of Je - sus,
I will give Him all my life.
As for

100
F♯m7
E/G♯
C
me, no mat - ter what the sac - ri - fice,
(cues optional)
103
Dsus
D
E
1.
2.
I will fol - low Christ.
I will
107
C
Dsus
D
E
grad. cresc.
I will fol - low Christ.
grad. cresc.
111
C
Dsus
D
C
Dsus
D
E
I will, I will fol - low Christ!

One Drop of Blood

Recorded by Ray Boltz

RAY BOLTZ

RAY BOLTZ and
STEVE MILLIKAN

10
C♯m
mp
B/C♯
1. Standin in' the court-room when I heard, "How do you plead?" The ac-
2. I stood and watched in si-lence as oth-ers were brought in; I
mp
12
C♯m
B/C♯
cus-er of the breth-ren was star-in' at me.
saw them start to trem-ble when they turned and faced their sin.
14
C♯m
B/C♯
He said, "We've got your num-ber, there is no es-cape,
They of-fered no ex-cus-es, they of-fered no al-i-bis.
16
C♯m
G♯sus
G♯
for here are your trans-gres-sions, your fail-ures and mis-takes."
The truth was o-ver-whelm-ing and it would not be de-nied.

18
F♯m7
C♯m/E
He point - ed to the cor - ner where the scales of jus - tice stood;
Their right-eous - ness like filth - y rags, and noth - in' they could say.
20
D♯m7(♭5)
G♯7/B♯
C♯m7
I saw so man - y fail - ures there, there was noth - ing good.
They bowed their heads in si - lence as they were led a - way.
22
F♯m7
C♯m/E
And in that ver - y mo - ment when it seemed all hope was lost, I said, "I
But for the true be - liev - ers, each time it was the same, His
24
A
Bsus
B
cresc.
f
plead the blood of Je - sus and His death up - on the cross." One drop of
glo - ry shone a-round them as they called up - on His name.
cresc.

26
E
F♯m
E/G♯
B sus
B
blood fell to the scales, it
28
F♯m
F♯m/E
B/D♯
C♯m7
B
cov - ered my trans - gres - sions for all the times I failed. The
30
E
F♯m
E/G♯
F♯m/A
F♯m7
F♯m/A
en - e - my was might - y, he came in like a flood;
32
E/B
B7sus
B7
he was de - feat - ed by one drop of

34
1.
C♯m
B/C♯
blood.
mf
36
C♯m
B/C♯
38
2.
E
G
building
D/F♯
blood.
No great - er sac - ri - fice has
building
40
E
A♭/E♭
E♭sus/D♭
E♭/D♭
an - y oth - er made.
Oh yes, He paid the price with

42
Csus
C
ff
F
Gm F/A
ev - 'ry drop He gave.
2nd time: blood.
ff
44
Csus
C
Gm
Gm/F
Fell to the scales, it cov - ered my trans - gres - sions for
46
C/E
Dm7
C
F
Gm F/A
all the times I failed. The en - e - my was might - y, he
48
Gm/B♭
Gm7
F/A
Gm/B♭
1.
F/C
came in like a flood; he was de - feat - ed by

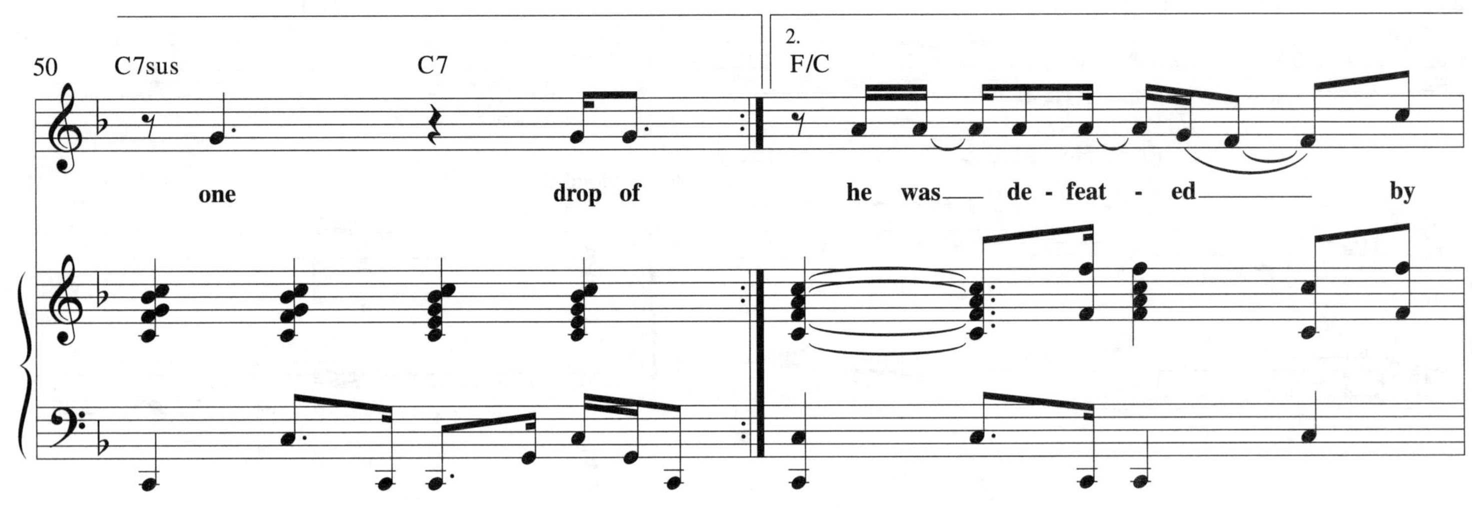
50
C7sus
C7
2.
F/C
one
drop of
he was — de - feat - ed — by

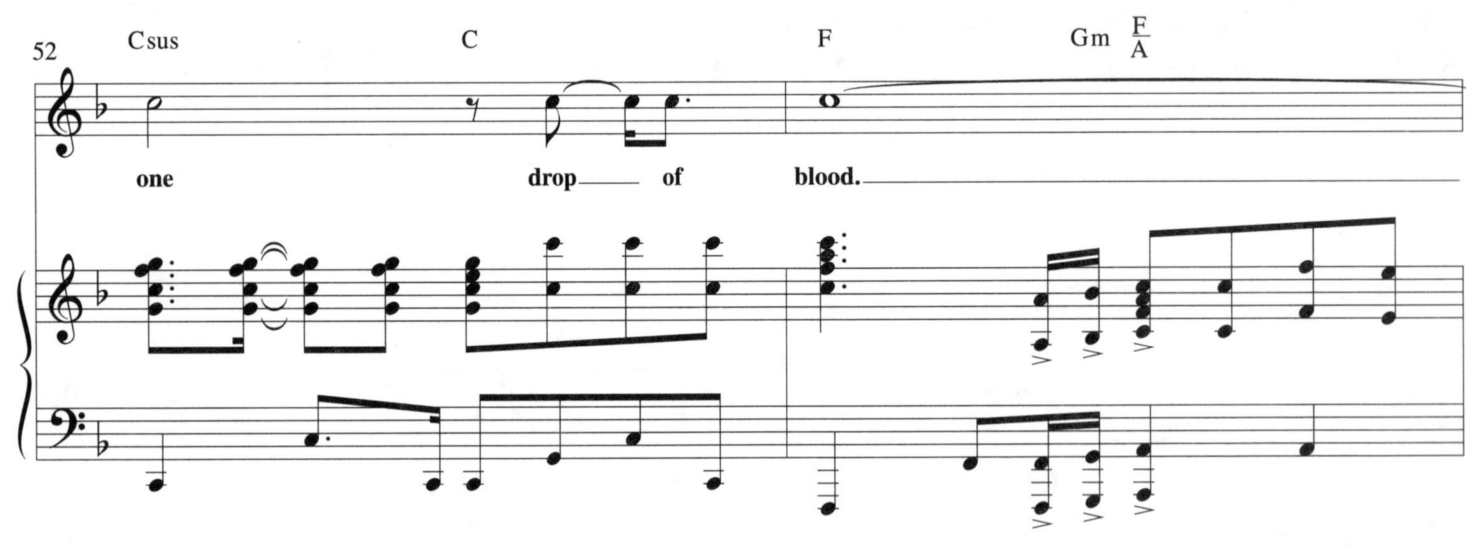
52
Csus
C
F
Gm
F/A
one
drop — of
blood. —

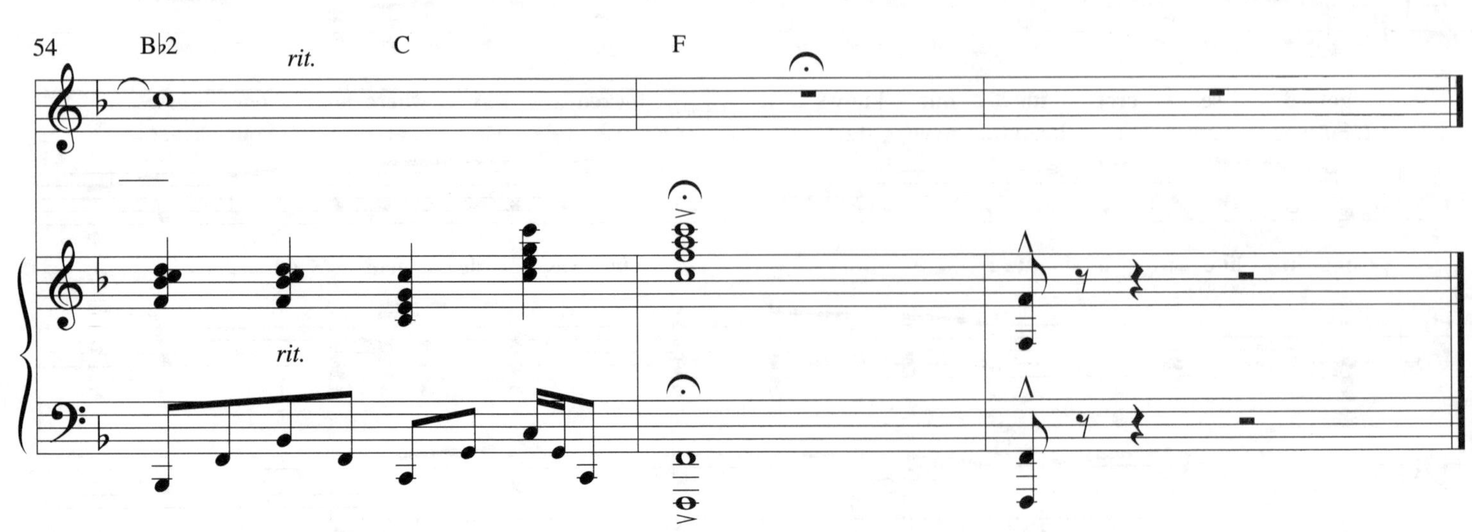
54
B♭2
rit.
C
F
rit.

I Am the Way

Recorded by Mark Schultz

Words and Music by
MARK SCHULTZ

11
Cmaj7
Bm/D
deep in - side your heart,
it's tear - in' you a - part.
You
down on bend - ed knee
for the world to see.
13
E(5)
Bm/D
hide the pain in all you do,
still the shack - les bind - ing you
are
And the chains a - round your heart
fall a - way and break a - part,
15
Cmaj7
Am7(♭5)
heav - i - er than stone,
but you are not a - lone.
sud - den - ly you see
the truth has set you free.
17
mf
G
D(4)/F♯
Em
D(4)
C
D(4)
G
D(4)/F♯
Em
When you're down look a - round and you'll see I am with you. Look to Me and you'll see I will

20
D(4) C D(4) G D(4)/F♯ Em D(4) C
be there to guide you. Take My hand and I can lead you on for you know:
23
G D/F♯ G/B C2 G D/A
f
I am the an - swer, and I am
26
G/B C2 G D/F♯ G/B C2
3rd time to Coda
the way, I am the prom - ise, and
29
G D/A
1.
C D G(5)
2.
C D G(5)
I have called your name. called your name. Sur -

32
C2
Em7(4)
G
D(5)
Bm
G/B
G2/B
round - ed by dark - ness you stum - bled a - long
know - ing the road that you
35
C2
Em7(4)
G
trav - eled was long.
But I'm here be - side you, yes,
37
D(5)
Bm
G
G2
here all a - long,
the one that will car - ry you
C2
C2(♯4)
C
D.S. al CODA
39
on.

CODA
43
G
D/F♯
C2
I have called.
Oh,
46
G(5)
D/F♯
G/B
C2
when you are down you think no one's a - round, but I'll
48
G(5)
D/F♯
G/B
C2
be with you both night and day.
50
G(5)
D/F♯
G/B
C2
I know the good times, I'll see you through bad times, oh,

52
G(5) D/F♯ G/B C2
you know that I'm here to stay.
54
G D/F♯ G/B C2 G D/A
I am the an - swer, and I am
f
57
G/B C2 G D/F♯ G/B C2
the way, I am the prom - ise, and
60
G D/A C2
I have called your name,

Vocal: 1st time only
63
G
D/F♯
G/B
C2
yeah,
your
name.
65
G
D/A
1.
G/B
C2
2.
67
C
D
C2/E
G
D(4)/F♯
Em
When you're down look a - round and you'll
69
C
D(4)
G
see I am with you.

I Will Be Your Friend

Recorded by Michael W. Smith

Words and Music by
MICHAEL W. SMITH
and CINDY MORGAN

With feeling ♩ = 90

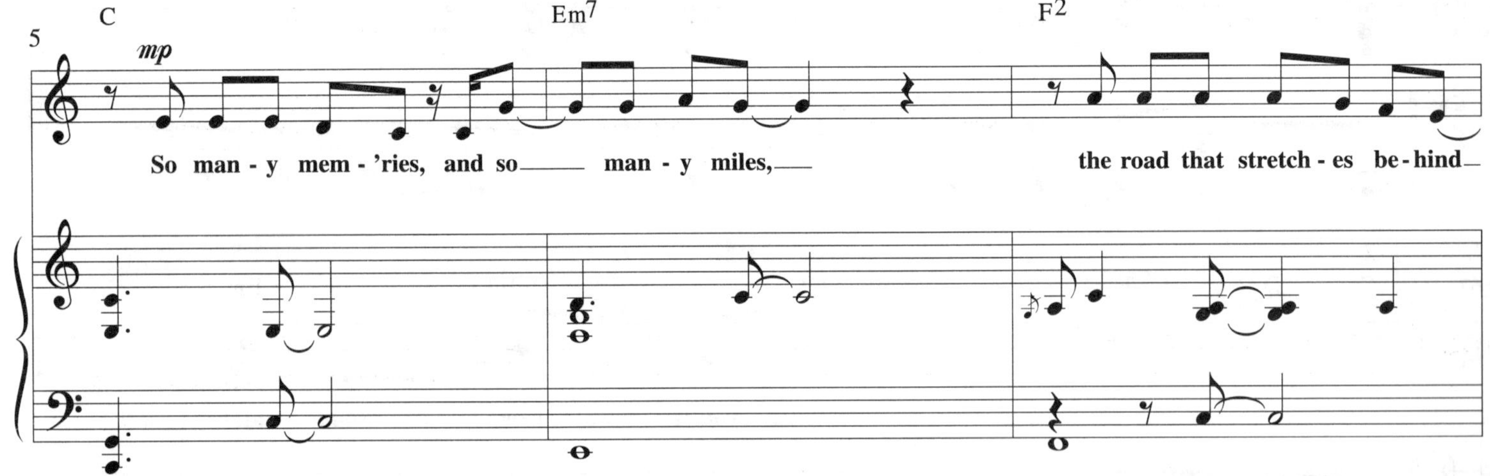

11
F2
E7sus
E7
Am
Em7
mf
but all these mo - ments u - nite us.
I'll be your friend for a life -
14
F
C/E
Am
Em7
F
E/G♯
- time,
a - gainst the wind and the rain
of ev - 'ry sea - son.
17
Am
Em7
F
C/E
Am
Cmaj9/E
Won't walk a - way in the hard times;
I will be your friend,
20
F
C/E
D/F♯
Fm6
C
I'm say - in', "I will be your friend."

23
Em7
F2
Dm9
G7sus
Da da da da dat da
26
C
Em7
F2
Sure as the riv - er runs to the sea,
high as the moun - tain that reach -
29
Dm9
G7sus
C
- es,
oh, you were there by my side
31
Em7
C
E
Em7
F2
Esus
E
'til the end,
and helped me on my feet a - gain.

34
Am
Em7
F
C/E
I'll be your friend for a life - time,
36
Am
Em7
F
E/G♯
Am
Em7
a - gainst the wind and the rain of ev - 'ry sea - son. Won't walk a - way in the hard
39
F
C/E
Am
Cmaj7/E
F
C/E
2nd time to Coda
times; I will be your friend, I'm say - in',
42
D/F♯
Fm6
C
G/B
"I will be your friend."

44
Am
E/G♯
So, in the val - ley, walk on, don't have to face it a - lone,
46
Am/G
D7/F♯
D7
'cause in the hard times we keep grow - in' strong; as we
48
F
C/E
Am
Cmaj7/G
learn, as we live that we
50
F
C/E
F2/A
E7/G♯
D.S. al CODA
live when we give.

CODA
52
D/F♯
Fm6
C
G/B
"I will be your friend."
54
Am
G6
F
C/E
D/F♯
Fm6
Oh, ah, I will be,
57
C
Em7
oh, your friend, yeah.
60
F
Dm9
molto rit.
A
Da da da da dat da Oh.
molto rit.

Lord of Eternity

Recorded by Fernando Ortega

Words and Music by
FERNANDO ORTEGA and
JOHN ANDREW SCHREINER

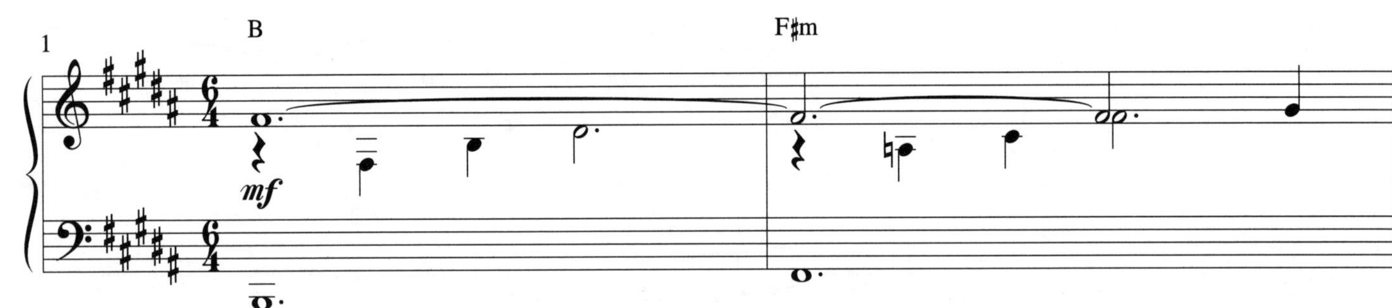

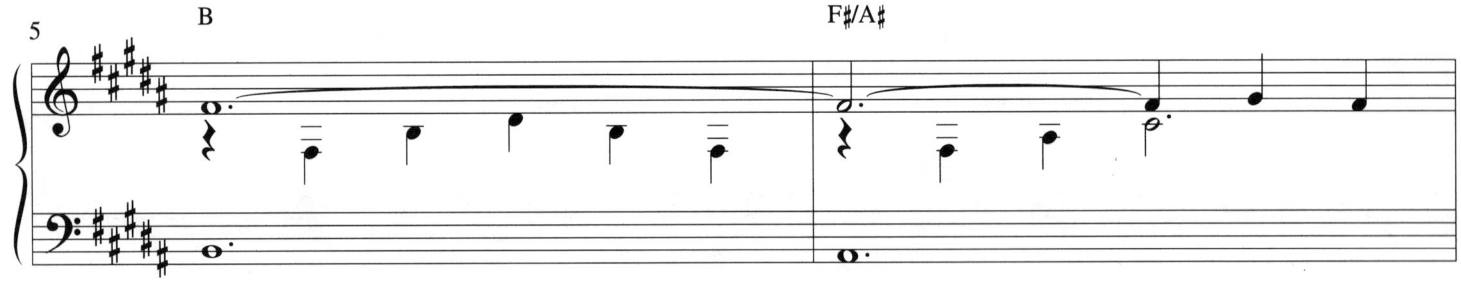

9
B
mp
Emaj7
1. Bless - ed is the man who walks in Your fa - vor,
mp
12
B
who loves all Your words and hides them like
15
Emaj7
C♯m
treas - ure. In the dark - est place
18
C♯m/B
F♯/A♯
E/G♯
of his des - p'rate heart, they are a light,

21
B/F♯
F♯
B
a strong, sure light.
25
mf
B2
2. Some - times I call out Your name, but I can - not
(3.) You are my de - fend - er, who is a -
mf
27
Emaj9
E2,6
find You.
gainst me?
I
29
B2
look for Your face, but You are not
No one can trou - ble or harm me if You are my

31
Emaj9
E2,6
C♯m
there.
By my
sor - rows, Lord,
strength.
All I
ask,
34
G♯m/B
F♯/A♯
E/G♯
lift me to You,
lift me up
all I de - sire,
is to live in Your
37
B/F♯
F♯
B2
to
Your
side.
house
all my
days.
40
Emaj9
Lord of e - ter - ni - ty,
Fa - ther of
2nd time God of all

43
G♯m7
Emaj9
mer - cy, look on my faint -
mer - cy, come to my trou -
46
F♯
G♯m
f
ing soul.
bled soul.
Keep - er of
49
Emaj9
G♯m7
all the stars, Friend of the poor - est heart,
f
52
Emaj7
F♯
2nd time to CODA
touch me and make me

55
B
F♯m
A2
whole.
mf
58
E/G♯
B
F♯/A♯
61
A2
E/G♯
D.S. al CODA
mf
3. If
CODA
63
B2
whole.
Lord of e - ter -

65
Emaj9
G♯m7
- ni - ty,
Fa - ther of
mer - cy,
68
Emaj9
F♯
come to my
trou
-
bled
71
G♯m
Emaj9
soul.
Keep - er of
all the stars,
74
G♯m7
Friend of the poor
-
est heart,
touch me and

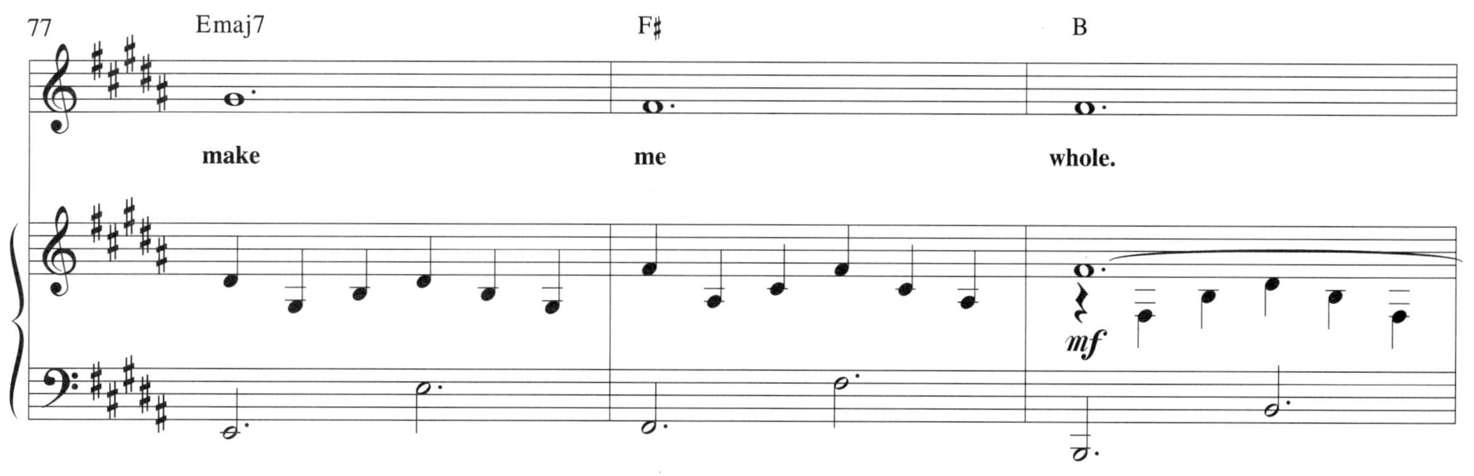
77
Emaj7
F♯
B
make
me
whole.
mf

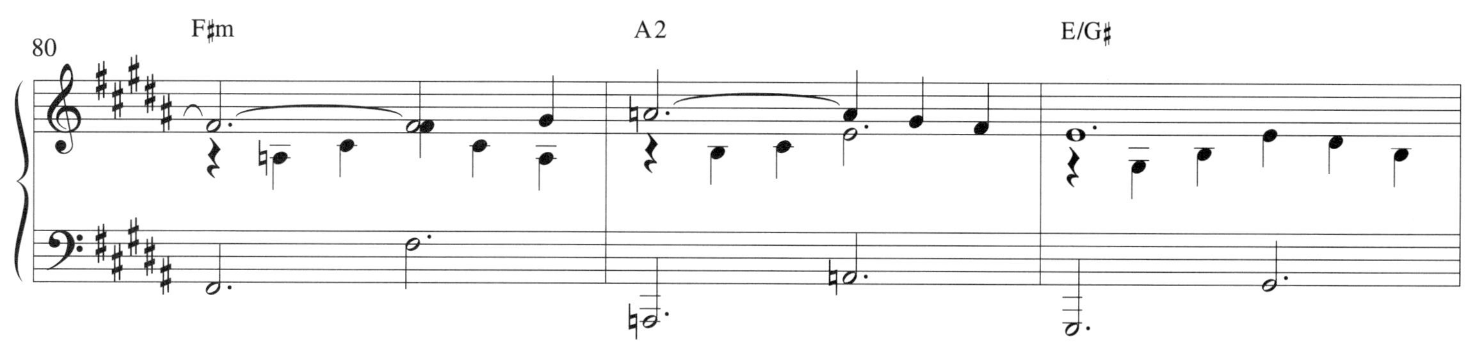
80
F♯m
A2
E/G♯

83
B
F♯/A♯

85
A2
E/G♯
B